THE HIGHWAY TO HEALING

SHAE PRATCHER

LIMITLESS LIGHT PRODUCTIONS STUDIOS LLC

CONTENTS

About the Author   v
Synopsis   vii
Dedication   ix
Introduction   xi

1. "Glance Back to Get Back"   1
2. "What Happened?"   9
3. "The Exchange"   14
4. "The Return"   18
5. "It Is What It Is"   24
6. "Little Man 606"   36
7. "Breakdown To Breakthrough"   53
8. "Stop, Settle, or Step?"   66
9. "Faith Fuel Stop"   75
10. "Detour is in The Details"   79
11. "Just Us"   83
12. "Trauma Triggered"   87
13. "The Sit Down"   91
14. "The Stand Up"   99
15. "It Is What It Is…Until You Do Something Different"   107
16. "The Long Handle Spoon Approach"   163
17. "Power in the U-Turn"   166
18. "The Highway to Healing" Exit   175

Author's Note & Acknowledgment   179

ABOUT THE AUTHOR

Shae'vada Pratcher, known to many as Shae, was born in Fairbanks, AK, but grew up in many states, being a military brat. She is co-founder and part owner of Limitless Light Productions Studios LLC with her husband.

She has made a name for herself in relation to radio through her podcast segment, "Let's Talk", under the umbrella of "Finding My Way Network", which broadcasted internationally. She was also a part of Atlanta's V1075 Radio Station Ministry with her show, "Praying Partners", where she encouraged, uplifted, and motivated many with her content. She also interviewed celebrities such as Erica Campbell of the Grammy Award-winning group Mary Mary and award-winning actress, Terri J. Vaughn.

She enjoys spending time with her family and friends and has a passion for singing. She is a proud member of the Gospel group, "Limitless", which released their first album, "Enter The Light", in 2018 across all major platforms.

The Highway to Healing is her first nonfiction book.

COPYRIGHT

Some names have been omitted to protect privacy.

The Highway to Healing. Copyright © 2023 by Shae Pratcher. All rights reserved. No portion of this book may be reproduced in any form without written permission from the publisher or author, except as permitted by US copyright law.

This publication is designed to provide accurate and authoritative information regarding the subject matter covered. It is sold with the understanding that neither the author nor the publisher is engaged in rendering legal, investment, accounting, or other professional services. While the publisher and author have used their best efforts in preparing this book, they make no representations or warranties with respect to the accuracy or completeness of the contents of this book and specifically disclaim any implied warranties of merchantability or fitness for a particular purpose. No warranty may be created or extended by sales representatives or written sales materials. The advice and strategies contained herein may not be suitable for your situation. You should consult with a professional when appropriate. Neither the publisher nor the author shall be liable for any loss of profit or any other commercial damages, including but not limited to special, incidental, consequential, personal or other damages.

Book Cover by Mazio Pratcher.

Library of Congress Cataloging-in-Publication Data has been applied for.

Published by Limitless Light Productions Studios LLC

ISBN 979-8-9876851-1-2

SYNOPSIS

The Highway to Healing is a representation of life's journey. A journey filled with experiences that encompass steep curves, wide, narrow, short and long pathways through beautiful scenic terrain. Yet and still, the highway has its hazards. Hidden shallow and deep potholes are common here. Adverse weather conditions may delay and/or reroute you. Rest stops along the way provide you with the time to reflect on past obstacles, new challenges, and future destinations. Being fueled by faith, courage, and strength will lead you to your destination of true healing.

While our journeys may not be exact, you may resonate with mine, and vice versa. It's important to understand that we can all learn something from each other, no matter the difference in age, gender, or any of that other stuff we put labels on. Be willing to bet on YOU, the HEALED YOU! I'm not talking about the "half healed" version of yourself where you confront what's comfortable to circumvent what's conducive. True healing requires commitment. You owe it to yourself. Too often we sacrifice ourselves, including our happiness, peace of mind, and joy, without ever being intentional about pouring back into our own cups.

"GIVE YOURSELF PERMISSION AND USE YOUR PAIN TO POUR INTO YOUR PATH THAT LEADS YOU TO YOUR PURPOSE."

~SHAE PRATCHER ~

DEDICATION

This book is dedicated to my husband, Mazio; our angel son in heaven, Braylen; our children, Jaylen, Janiyah & Justus; and all trauma survivors.

This book is for anyone who has ever experienced trauma. The way we internalize it is different, but ultimately, it impacts us well into our adulthood. There are triggers each of us will experience that have no boundaries. They come at the most inopportune times, and when we least expect it, forcing us to relive the pain repeatedly.

My hope is that we grow beyond our fears and break free from the silence to allow ourselves to heal for real. While my journey may not be identical to yours, I want to encourage you to step, despite your struggles or situation. You don't have to suffer in silence anymore. Your voice matters and has the power to change lives!

Those who have wronged us tend to want to control the narrative so that it is more easily digested and comfortable for them. We have been forced to deal with the choices of others, despite how it's made us feel, but we can reclaim our power by speaking our truth out loud. There's healing in helping others, and in the process, you continue to GROW. Nothing real can be threatened, so live in your truth for the rest of your days! Roll the dice and bet on YOU!

INTRODUCTION

It is my prayer that you are:
  D - Dedicated to your healing journey.
  I - Inspired by the freedom that comes from sharing your testimony and encouraging others.
  C - Consistent with being intentional about making the choice to choose YOU!
  E - Empowered to make a difference by living in your truth and holding YOU accountable.

Chapter 1
Glance Back To Get Back

"So, how did we get here?" This question was one I struggled with as I sat on my therapist's sofa in the well put together office space. I felt safe. I didn't know what to expect, so I took a deep breath and gave it a shot.

"We are here because we are at a crossroads in our marriage, and I feel like this is the only thing we have not tried."

I remember drowning in my thoughts and waiting with anticipation as his eyes searched for the right words to answer her question from his perspective. In my mind, I had it all figured out. We were here because, once again, he hadn't chosen me and had been communicating with another female in a context that I did not appreciate as his wife.

I couldn't help but further make my point by explaining, "He tends to be at a loss of words when it comes to talking about the things he does when he is in the wrong."

He agreed he messed up and said he wanted to make things work between us, but for me, it wasn't good enough. I wanted the therapist to make him give me the reason he continued to do these things. I wanted comfort and a peace of mind, knowing our marriage was special. I wanted to feel protected, but instead, I felt used and stuck. I wanted to trust him above all these things.

Before he could say anything else, I was ready to respond to any excuse or explanation had because this was a cycle that had continued to haunt us in our years together.

Instead, he said, "There is no excuse for what I did. I was wrong and I want to do better and know that I can be a better man for you and our family. I don't want to lose you."

In reality, it was deeper than any answer either of us had given, and she knew it.

Amid the laundry list of comebacks we had at the ready, they were not each other's best qualities. She challenged us to be more intentional about sharing positive feedback about each other, with each other, and be ready to discuss at our next session.

We arrived at the next session with a sense of readiness that we both felt without expressing it vocally. Walking into the office, we felt good and were ready to unpack the heavy load we had been carrying for so long. She asked for our affirmations that we were to be intentional about for the week, and we shared them out loud with each other. Then she jumped back into the previous week's notes to pick up where we left off.

She asked if we had spoken in greater detail about the specific incident that had brought us to the point of deciding therapy was the best approach. I explained we had not because he was not ready to discuss it. I expressed my frustration in this because I did not feel it was fair that he could control when we had a discussion about something he'd done that had caused me great distress.

She said, "You must respect each other's boundaries. While he does have a responsibility to talk through what transpired, give him time to process everything and come to you when he is ready."

"That's never going to happen if we put the ball in his court," I replied.

She turned to him and asked, "Can you be committed to circling back to her once you are ready to discuss the details of what transpired?"

He replied, "Yes, I can do that."

She further explained that in listening during our first couple of sessions, she realized I was a fast thinker and could respond quickly. While that worked for me, he wasn't the same way, and I shouldn't expect him to respond quickly whenever I presented a problem to him. She asked me to be committed to giving him time and allowing him to communicate when he was ready, and I agreed.

She commended us both for standing on our commitments and being open and willing to adjust accordingly, and challenged us to continue to be intentional with our affirmations to each other. We wished her well until our next session.

As we parted this session, we did something we had not done until that point. We had a conversation about the therapy session we had left. We shared how much we appreciated and enjoyed the sessions.

Later that week, my husband came back to me and said he was ready and willing to talk about his choice that led us to therapy. We were able to speak candidly about what transpired and he owned the fact that he should not have entertained the text message from the female he worked with when it was received, but he had. He further assured me it had nothing to do with what I was doing or had not done. He had just made a bad decision by responding and had no intentions of things going further. He did it for attention.

He owned the fact that the context of the messages were not appropriate for a married man. He acknowledged my feelings and allowed me the opportunity to explain why I was so unhappy with what had transpired. I explained to him that there was no comfort in feeling like, at any moment, your spouse could reach out and entertain other women just because. I advised him I made a conscious choice every day to be faithful to him simply because it was the commitment I made. I told him it wasn't hard for me to do and it shouldn't be hard for him to understand where I was coming from.

I cried and explained that I was tired of living and feeling as though I had to take what everyone else gave me. I hadn't done anything to deserve it, yet I was always the one getting the short end of the stick.

He empathized with me and asked, "What will it take for you to trust me again?"

I replied, "I honestly don't know anymore. I don't have the right answers. I just know I am tired of feeling like this, tired of crying, and I am over it. Besides walking away, I don't have any more answers, so I need to pray and seek God."

He apologized and stated he was willing to do whatever it took, he just didn't want to lose his family. He assured me he understood the amount of undue stress he had placed on me over the years, and therefore, would respect whatever decision I made as a result of his choices.

We left the conversation there so I could have time to pray and talk to God before our next therapy session.

They say the third time is a charm and I must agree. We showed up, and while I felt drained from crying, praying, and trying to figure out what I wanted, I was ready.

The therapist welcomed us back and made a few jokes about the fact we had shown up again, which was a good sign. We laughed.

She asked us to talk about our week and confirm that we had been intentional with our affirmations for each other. We advised we had been intentional for most of the week, but fell off toward the end of the week. She wanted to understand why this had been and we explained the week had been hectic and I was processing some things. She probed further to understand what had transpired since our last session.

She started the session off this time, asking my husband to share his thoughts on how the week had gone. He explained he had circled back with me to further discuss the events of the situation with the lady from work that he'd had inappropriate conversations with. He went into detail about what he took from the conversation and how I responded. She wanted his take on my response.

He explained, "I actually understood exactly what she was saying, and I agree with whatever decision she makes."

She asked him, "What would you like to see happen?"

He replied, "I would definitely like to stay with my family. I don't want to lose them. They mean everything to me."

The therapist turned to me and asked, "How are you feeling?"

I was empty at that moment and told her, "I feel all cried out. To be honest, I hear what he is saying, but we have been here before. He says I am sorry, and I want to be with you, but goes out and entertains these women who mean nothing, at the end of the day. There is no comfort in what is happening to me. I shared this with him, and I will share it with you. I feel stuck. I feel like I am supposed to just take whatever people give to me and I am over it.

"On one hand, of course, I want my marriage to work, but I just don't feel as though he will ever choose me. That's what hurts the most for me. I want him to do right by me simply because it's the right thing to do. Not be sorry because he got caught or because he feels like he has to because it's convenient."

Tears flowed at this point, so she handed me a tissue. I looked over and saw this look on my husband's face that I had never seen before. It was a true, sincere, apologetic look that came from deep within.

The therapist turned to him and asked, "What is your response to what she is saying to you in this moment?"

He replied, "I know I have let you and the family down. Honestly, I am letting myself down because I know I can be a better man. I know I can give you what you deserve. All I can hope and ask for is that you find it within yourself to forgive me and let me show you better than I can tell you because I know we have been here before. I am sorry I hurt you. You don't deserve it. I love you, and I am willing to do whatever it takes to get us back on the right path."

She asked me, "Are you willing to give him time to show you he can change and be the man he knows he can be for you?"

I replied, "All I can do is pray and let God lead me, to be honest. I can't make any promises because, as much as I want it to work, I must trust God."

She said she felt this was fair, then she explained she wanted to change direction and learn a bit more about our childhood. She asked some questions about my immediate family and did the same for my husband. We answered the questions, and this was where we learned we had a lot more to unpack than we'd ever imagined.

For me, I had made a promise to myself that I would be truthful about whatever was asked of me in order to get to the root cause of our marital issues. In this, we uncovered that a lot of the ways I communicate, respond, and feel are derived from my childhood trauma. I am more vocal due to the lack of voice I had growing up.

Growing up in a military household had its challenges. It was strict. I did not have nearly as much freedom as my brothers had. The leash was so tight, there was no room for anything extra. We had nice things, and I don't remember a time where my needs weren't fulfilled. Additionally, I learned as a kid there was a lack of time and effort put forth in spending quality time. While many may believe this does not impact the way you raise your family, it does.

Through therapy sessions, we learned that due to my husband's mother not raising him and struggling with addiction, this presented its own set of challenges. Abandonment issues and rebellion were two of the things that were birthed from the childhood trauma of not having his mama around.

Together, we also explained the tragic loss of our first-born son, Braylen Makai Pratcher. There are some scars that can never be fully healed to a point of no detection.

The therapist looked us in our eyes and explained that the fact we were still together spoke volumes. She encouraged us that we didn't have a bad marriage and the things we were experiencing were not irreconcilable unless we wanted them to be. We were assured that she had met with couples in much worse states with real issues that required a miracle. We had some work to do, sure, and she recommended individual counseling to really unpack, confront, and address the childhood traumas we both endured, but there was hope. The therapist said she was confident that once we made the choice to do this, we would grow better together because we'd understand so much more about ourselves. There were a few more questions about my circumstances and she confirmed for me I needed to reconsider my environment as it was not normal and almost impossible to heal in dysfunction. This was something that resonated with me so much, it kept playing over and over in my head.

(We walked away with a common understanding that the only way this was going to work was if we were both dedicated to confronting our childhood trauma.)

We had gotten here because we failed to realize the importance of glancing back at where we had come from to truly understand what was still there that had been left unresolved. The only way to get back on track is to be intentional about dealing with your past.

We had help to recognize there were flaws in the foundation we had started from. The same things we chose to overlook would continue to resurface. We couldn't escape it and needed to embrace it as it was what made us who we are.

"The one thing I have always admired about our relationship and marriage is we have always been willing to fight for what we want. Against all odds, we have made a choice to be the difference we want to see in the chaos, understanding that neither one of us is perfect. We have flaws and things that make us unique individuals, but the one common thing we have is our love for each other and the willpower to do what it takes to make it work.

Chapter 2

What Happened?

I was a young, innocent, carefree little girl with such a bright and promising future. I remember it like it was yesterday. I was loving and living life while taking every day in stride with everything it offered.

I lived with my biological parents and two brothers growing up. Over the years, we moved around a lot due to both parents being in the military, which made it difficult to make long-term friends. We stayed with family members for a few deployments while our parents were away. Throughout the years, our family had its challenges, like any other family. The biggest obstacles within our family were the lack of time our parents were able to spend or invest into me and my brothers and the communication between my mother and me.

She was the only girl growing up and I was the only girl within the household growing up, so you would think the bond would be strong. I don't really remember the exact time where the shift happened, but it did. Once this happened, the verbiage she used to grasp my attention was in poor taste, in my opinion. I had been called the B-word, along with a host of other profane names. Honestly, although it hurt my feelings at times, I can't say that I internalized it until I got older. I actually grew to expect it and became numb, not thinking twice when it did occur. My father would come to my rescue and did his best to neutralize the verbal abuse at times.

One day was all it took to change everything and the world as I knew it was never the same again.

My mom was away, and my brothers were out, enjoying their friends like any other day. It was just him and me at the house. I was around seven or eight at the time. He came to my room and asked me to come downstairs. We watched TV and ate just the same as we would any other day. Then, he said he wanted to teach me some things so other little boys could not take advantage of me. He advised me that there was no "hanky panky" and said we should keep it between us.

He started off by showing me his private part. He explained to me what "it" was, and that girls and boys had different private parts. He touched my parts and reiterated this. I thought nothing of it.

The second time, I remember him taking his private part out of his pants and stroking it up and down until semen came out of it. He explained to me that was what could get me pregnant. Prior to any of these interactions, he was very intentional about stating he was only teaching me and there was no "hanky panky".

Over time, the conversations and interactions escalated. If I was sitting on his lap, watching TV, he would do things like make his private part jump or move to where I could feel it on my butt or leg. This would happen if others were in the room or not. Then, there were nights where my mom would have duty or had to go to the field and those nights were the worse.

He would close my brothers' room door, come into my room, and get into my bed. Initially, he would just come and lay in my bed next to me. From there, he would lay me on top of him so that his private area was aligned with mine. Although he had on boxers and I had on my night clothes, I could feel the imprint of his private part. He then thrust his hips so that his private part would grind against my body with clothes on. This happened countless times over the course of a couple of years.

As I got older and my body changed, he would kiss me in the mouth and touch my breasts and explain that if I wanted them to be bigger, I would need to play with them. Things escalated even further, and he started having me stroke his private part until he climaxed. Then, he would suck on my breasts. This happened more times than I could count.

Many nights, he would come in and start licking my private parts. This happened frequently, even with my mom being home, sleeping in their bed. He had me suck his private many times, and one day, the semen got in my mouth. I wanted to throw up. I gagged and remembered crying.

There was a time where I gathered the courage and voiced that I did not like it and did not want to participate in these interactions. He would get upset and say things about going out and cheating on my mom and he would advise me we would both be in trouble if I ever decided to speak about it.

There was a time when I was a teenager when he made his first attempt to put his private part inside of mine. I was so scared. He placed it up against mine during that session and stroked himself until semen ran down my private part.

The next month, I was late coming on my period. I remember him telling me not to tell my mom. Instead, he told me to do exercises, especially sit-ups and crunches and to drink milk. I eventually did come on my period, it was just late. By this time, I felt things were way out of control and didn't know what to do or who could help me. I had poor hygiene from showering less, hoping if he came in during the night, this would dissuade him from going down on me. It did not work. He did not care and would proceed with what his goal was when he came into my room.

I remember feeling disgusted, scared, and helpless, among so many other emotions. Just when I believed things could get no worse, it did. He started calling me to "help him" in different areas of the house while my brothers or mom were home and requested I go down on him.

A day that stands out in my memory is when he called me downstairs to the basement. He already had a washcloth ready so he could catch the semen instead of letting it go in my mouth. This became a routine. A couple of times, he used a vibrator on my private part. These things happened to me repeatedly for about seven years and in multiple houses that we lived in throughout that time.

The last straw was a day that I remember so clearly, around the age of fifteen. It was etched in my mind, and I would never forget it.

My mother was not there and he had woken us all up. He had a yard task for my brothers and demanded they rake all the leaves and bag them prior to coming back inside the house.

He locked the door and had me lay on the kitchen floor, near the stove. He had a condom and wanted to take my virginity. I was so scared; I was shaking.

As he tried to get it in, I broke down crying. I remember one of my brothers trying to get in the house. He was so mad, he went and exchanged words with him and came back to me, attempting to put it in again and became irate over my reaction.

He got up and told me, "I bet if I was one of them little knucklehead boys, you wouldn't have a problem." It was at that very moment, I realized I had to tell somebody. I had to get out of this cycle. It was breaking me down and I couldn't even think straight. I was not the normal, happy, carefree teenager I should have been.

I built up the courage and made a choice to tell my older brother's girlfriend at the time. I told her everything. I wanted help. I needed help. She empathized and assured me it was going to be OK, but expressed that I had to tell my older brother. I was desperate and knew it was what I had to do. I told my older brother all about what I had been experiencing for the past seven years and he assured me it was going to be OK.

The next morning, there was a loud knock on the door. There were some very familiar voices, and I knew I was being rescued. All of my mom's brothers were there to help me. One of my uncles came to my room and told me this would be one of the hardest, if not the hardest, things I would ever have to do. He explained he was going to bring my mother into my room and he needed me to share everything with her. He brought her to my room and left us to discuss what I'd been suffering through silently.

Chapter 3
The Exchange

There were so many emotions as I struggled to find the words to say to my mom. Emotionally, I was a wreck. I was scared, nervous, and didn't know what to expect after I shared this life-changing information with her.

What I was sure of was that I needed her unconditional love in that moment to feel safe and secure.

My mom came into my room that day to a heartbroken daughter who needed her more than ever. I remember crying through it but explaining to her how much I had experienced in seven years. I felt disgusted, embarrassed, and ashamed the entire time I shared the details with her.

There was dead silence, and a thickness that filled the air that was eerie. It only lasted for a few minutes, but it felt like forever.

She sighed deeply and I will never forget the first words that came from her lips on that day.

She said, "Describe it."

In that moment, I felt more pain and brokenness than I ever had in my entire life. After everything I had shared with her, it came down to her asking me to describe what his penis looked like. My heart sank after it skipped a few beats. I felt like she didn't believe me, and honestly, nothing could have prepared me for that response. Beyond anything I had experienced, this exchange between my mother and me cut deep. This conversation changed the dynamic of our relationship forever.

I described it for her, and she wanted to know when these encounters happened. We went through all the details and I explained it would happen when she was in the field, working late, and even when she was in her room, asleep at times. There was more silence just before she got up and left my room. I followed her and we walked down the stairs and into the living room where all my uncles and my dad were. There was a silence so thick as she walked straight to the kitchen and grabbed a knife. My dad looked so confused and lost as to what was going on.

She attempted to go after him with the knife, but my uncles stopped her. Things were blurry for me during the exchange leading up to this next part that cut even deeper than I could imagine.

Once my uncles were able to calm my mother down, it was understood that we needed to address the reason they were there. When everyone finally confronted my dad about what he had been doing to me, he looked at me with a straight face and said, "Shae, I never touched you."

My heart stopped, and for the first time in my life, I knew what it was like to have my breath leave me suddenly. All the tears I had cried in silence, all the nights I feared him coming in to do what had become "normal", all the years taken... stolen... snatched... flashed before me. I was a mess and speechless. I felt betrayed on so many levels. I was ready and willing to take a lie detector test.

My uncles stood ten toes down for me and escorted him right out the front door. For once in my life, I felt safe. I released a sigh of relief, thinking I could sleep through a night now without wondering and watching my door slowly open. Little did I know, that would be short-lived.

The weeks following were rough for me. Watching my mother walk around, moping, was depressing. I just wanted the abuse to stop. I didn't want to make waves within our family or cause her to be unhappy.

He communicated with us during the time he was not living in the house. She allowed him to talk to me. He apologized to me one day and said he understood why I told. He told me he was happy I had because things had gotten out of control, and he didn't know how to stop himself. He said not to worry and that he wasn't mad at me. I wanted my mom to hear this, so I tried to put the phone closer and put it on speakerphone, but she didn't want to hear it and refused to listen. Deep inside, I knew she knew I was telling the truth. I heard the conversations between them and arguments where she explained, "It's hard to describe something you never saw."

There were three individual discussions that happened between my mother, myself, and my brothers approximately three weeks after everything was brought to light. It was presented to us as a crossroads we had approached, and we needed to decide as a family. She asked if we wanted to move on without him or allow him to come back home. This was very different, as any decisions made up to that point, no matter how small or big, as kids, we had no say so in it. She made sure to stress that if we chose to move forward without him, then life would change drastically for us. We would have to downsize and have less than what we had at that point. The scene had already been set as to what we could expect if we continued the path we were on without him.

I thought about the options and there wasn't a lot of time to decide. I thought about how unhappy she had been since he had left, I thought about the damaged relationship she and I already had, and how much worse things could get for me if I made the "wrong" choice, and I thought about being the blame for my brothers not having a better life and having less because of what happened to me. In reality, all I wanted was for the abuse to stop so I could try to live a normal, happy life.

We chose to allow her to be happy and made the decision that he could come back. All I wanted was peace of mind, knowing he would leave me alone and never touch me or ask me to touch him again. She assured me that this would be the case, and that if I struggled when he came back, we could talk about it anytime.

During her conversation with me, she mentioned she wasn't trying to make any excuses, but wanted to share that he had been molested as a child. There was sympathy in her voice when she spoke about what happened to him, but none pertaining to what happened to me. I never understood that. To this day, I must realize it's a loose end that I will never wrap my mind around when it comes to her logic.

Chapter 4
The Return

He came back. We were back in the same shared space, and I was scared. I knew he would be upset and I didn't know what he was capable of. He was intentional about reminding me that things were not always the way they ended, and that it all started with him trying to "teach me" so other boys didn't take advantage of me. He was adamant that this was innocent, and things went too far. I didn't want to talk, think, or be reminded about that part of my life. It was still fresh. It wasn't fair to me the way any of this was unfolding. I was being forced to face this man again.

As for my mom, she still had to work. She still had to leave me there. I couldn't help but wonder, *What am I supposed to do? How am I supposed to feel?*

As for me, I smiled and minded all my manners and was determined to "Fake It Until I Make It". It was the only way. I no longer had allies, in my opinion. I had to figure out the way ahead, understanding I was on my own. I told myself I only had a few years left until I was eighteen and would be graduating. I started planning to get a job and save money to move out shortly after. I didn't discuss my plan with many people.

Things quieted down externally, but internally, there was turmoil. I found it hard to focus at school but knew that low grades were not acceptable, so I pushed myself every day.

One day, I was so overwhelmed with him being back and I was uncomfortable as he continued to have side bar conversations to apologize and reiterate the point that he was not mad at me and was happy I told. I had heard it so many times, it forced me to continuously relive it.

I decided to take my mom up on her offer and talk with her about what I was feeling. I explained to her I was uncomfortable and didn't know how to deal with it. During the conversation, she became irritated, and it showed in her tone and body language.

She advised, "I'm just going to turn myself in to my commander and take whatever punishment comes with it because you just aren't going to let this go. It's going to continue to come up, so I am probably going to go to jail, but it is what it is."

I was on an emotional rollercoaster at this point. I didn't know what to say, so I didn't say much. She made a few phone calls, and the next thing I remember was being on the phone with my grandfather. I paced back and forth on the sidewalk in front of our house as I listened to him.

My grandfather empathized with me regarding the way I felt and validated all the emotions I shared with him. He also explained that my mom had spoken to him and told him she was going to turn herself in, and he wanted to make sure I understood what that meant. My grandfather said my mom would go to jail at this point, and I wanted to understand how since she wasn't the one who had violated me for all those years. I didn't want anyone to go to jail, I just didn't know how to deal with the stress and issues I faced. He assured me he understood, but because my mother had been made aware of the situation and allowed my father to come back into the household, she would be responsible for child neglect, child endangerment, and potentially other charges. I started crying and remembered feeling stuck, like no matter what, I would have to deal with this for the rest of my life.

My grandfather explained that the choice was up to me, but molestation was hard to prove because he never "entered" me. He told me my father might get off and my mom would still end up being responsible, due to the allegations alone.

After listening to him, I said, "This is not the outcome I want. I will just deal with it."

I loved and respected my grandfather and we all looked up to him. We knew he was the solid part of our family and took advice from him to heart. I didn't want anything bad to happen and really didn't want anyone to get in trouble, but I wanted to feel safe and protected. The fact was, I wasn't and, unfortunately, once again, I had been robbed of this option.

I went back to my mom and asked her not to turn herself in because I did not want her to go to jail. I told her I would just deal with it.

My grandmother and I became really close during this time. My grandmother was very spiritual. She was able to really connect with me and allowed me to confide in her countless times. It was she who ended up buying me my very first Teen Bible. She was available most of the time when I needed her and we had a conversation that changed my path.

She told me, "Sometimes in life, we are dealt a hand that just doesn't seem fair. There is no explanation for the why behind this, but God trusts some of the biggest tests with His most precious children. While I can't explain to you why you are dealing with this, I know God has a plan. This won't make sense today, baby, but in the right time in your life, one day, it will. I can't tell you when that will be, but I will be right here, praying with you through it. I don't understand why the decisions are being made the way they have been, but know that God is always listening and never sleeping. He sees all, and trust me, nobody gets away with anything. We all reap what we sow.

"It's important that you do what you're supposed to and talk to God anytime, about anything. People will fail you, but God will never leave nor forsake you. When you are feeling lonely, lost, angry, sad, misled, disappointed, and anything in between, just open your Bible, baby, and read His word."

I cried and thanked my grandmother. She poured into me when no one else did. She was able to get through to me, and this was where my faith journey began.

When I went to her home, she took me to church faithfully. She made sure that if nothing else, I knew the Lord, and the power that lived within me because I had Him. For once, I felt like I was going to be able to press on one more day. That turned into days, weeks, months, and years.

The exact timeframe that passed is not coming to me, but it wasn't a long time before another conversation transpired between my mother and me. In this conversation, she asked, "Would you be willing to tell your uncles the abuse never happened?"

I looked in her face and told her, "No, because it did happen. That's not something I am going to be able to do."

This was another burn mark that was etched in my heart, and I'd carried for years for more reasons than one.

When I left that conversation, I was numb. It was probably the second time in my life I had stood up for myself. I felt betrayed and let down again. It was like a nightmare I could not escape.

At this time, I laid across my bed and cried. I remember talking to God and asking Him to please just let me make it until I graduate so I could move out and never look back. I didn't feel like, as kids, we ever had a voice in anything. We were the army brats who knew to do what we were told or else there would be consequences.

I remember a promise I made to myself that day. I promised I would never lie to anyone about what happened to me. If I was asked, I would tell the truth every single time. The fact that she would ask me to go back and lie to my uncles to make them feel comfortable about the choice they made to stay together really scarred me bad.

I grew to learn that the very ones who were supposed to protect me, did not protect me, and it is what it is. I couldn't help but think of the countless times I was sacrificed by them. They were supposed to love and protect me from others, but this wasn't the case. It was the biggest "secret" and keeping it that way was more important than my well-being.

The way we were raised did not allow me to show how I actually felt internally. I knew I had to smile and act like everything was fine. Due to the stress I felt, I shared what happened to me with a few friends, and I was sure my brothers did the same.

I had a boyfriend at the time who I ended up confiding in regarding what happened to me, and he was enraged by the information I had shared with him. He wrote me a letter, and I don't remember the exact words, but he threatened to hurt this man for what he did.

When I came home from school that day, it was "backpack check" day, which was a random thing my parents did. They would have us drop our backpacks off before we take them to our room and search them for anything (electronics, letters, etc.). I had letters in my backpack, including that specific one. She read them to him that night while she was in her room.

Within a few days, I remember her making a comment along the lines of, "Do you really think that little boy could do anything to hurt him?"

I was grounded. Although I didn't want anything bad to happen to anyone, it felt like the only people who could be compassionate and relate to me were not my family. Being young and stressed, I needed an outlet. I learned quickly they did not want us sharing the details of what transpired with anyone. We were reminded that what happened in this house, stayed in this house.

It wasn't right away when he returned, but within a few years, I was tasked with cleaning the fungus out of his toes and using tweezers to pick the ingrown hairs from his face. The nasty, smelly white fungus from wearing those army boots all those years still has a place in my memory bank. The ingrown hairs were such a nuisance, and I can remember hearing him breathe as he laid on my lap with his eyes closed. Blood oozed from the affected area on multiple occasions. These two tasks became a part of a routine for years. I couldn't help but think this was punishment or backlash for speaking up about what he had done. Whether this was the intent or not, it affected me, and I grew a true disgust for both tasks. To this day, I hate feet and the mere thought of deep cleaning mine, or anyone else's, is enough to make me hate life.

No one cared enough to get me or him, for that matter, any help throughout the years. There were no expectations or boundaries set. We were all pushed right back into the fire to figure it out as we went. I do believe that not attending counseling did more damage.

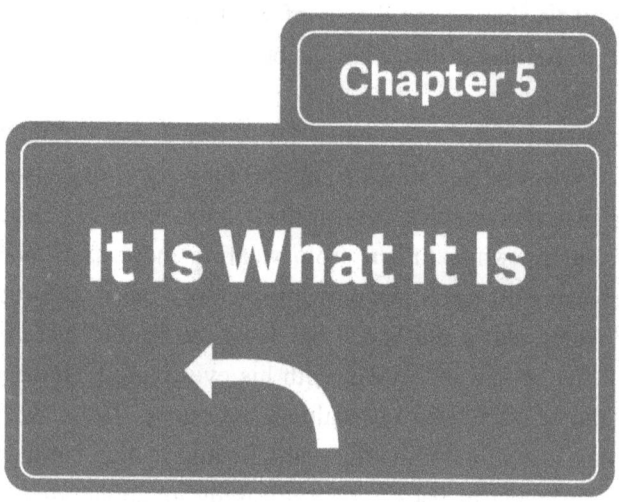

Chapter 5

It Is What It Is

There comes a time in life where you feel you are surviving. I had reached that point during my high school years. I had slowly distanced myself without even noticing it. I had to push the pain down and do other things to try to keep my mind from going to the hurtful memories. I couldn't determine what pain was worse: the sexual abuse or the fact I had no ally or outlet in my household.

I remember feeling numb and invisible. No one cared enough to take a stand and see it for what it was. I felt like I was the black sheep, especially after I spoke out about what happened.

"It is what it is" was a phrase I adopted as a coping mechanism. If you think on a traumatic experience or a time when you've been let down repeatedly, what was yours? It's natural for us to want to hurry up and get over, get through, or let it go. In my experience, this pressure to do so before I was ready had been intensified by the people who didn't understand my pain but also had contributed to my pain which was unfair.

Being young and feeling as though my life was spiraling way out of control was an understatement for me. The fear of what could or would happen to me if I got out of line kept me in check. I remember I strategized my exit plan. School was my outlet, and my friends were my escape. When I was anywhere but home, I felt safer. I couldn't do much outside of school with my friends, which was uncomfortable, and hard to explain. I found I had one best friend, and our time together was very limited. I confided in the circle of people I trusted and found comfort in that.

In time, I felt like things were getting "normal" for me and took solace in the fact the sexual abuse had stopped. My smile was coming back, and I blended in as much as I could. We had multiple family gatherings, which were very uncomfortable, as one could imagine. It was embarrassing to me that everyone knew what happened and my mother had taken him back. It was always weird to me how things just went back to normal. We would all get together, eat good, laugh, and go our separate ways. I was ashamed for a long time. It hurt that the ones who wanted to protect me had no control, either. I felt stuck.

I was around sixteen when my parents decided to move a young male soldier into our home. We all became really close and looked at him as another big brother. I was happy in a way because I felt like this was another layer of protection for me. Even though this man didn't know what happened to me, I felt better knowing he was there. We had many laughs, watched TV, and wrestled with each other occasionally. It was fun times. This happened and became a norm, and life was good.

I was home alone one day, laying on the couch, taking a nap. The male soldier came in and went on, doing what he typically did any other day. Then, he came into the living room and sat next to me, but very close to me. It was so quiet in the house, and what happened next caught me completely off guard. I felt his hands slide into my pants and his finger glided across my private part, into my hole. He repeatedly shifted his finger inside of me. I started crying. I couldn't even look at him. He asked me if I wanted him to stop and assured me he would if I wanted.

I said, "Yes, stop," and he did. He walked away, went upstairs, and I remember feeling overwhelmed with emotions again.

What do I do? How is this happening to me again? Is anyone even going to believe me? Like, why am I going through these things?

Amid all these questions, one thing was for sure—I wasn't willing to let this happen to me repeatedly. I couldn't do that to myself.

Shortly after the incident, my father came home. Then, all my other family members trickled in from their day of activities.

I told immediately this time what happened to me with the young soldier. There was a weird feeling that came over me because, what were they going to do? I had not gotten over what had happened to me since the age of seven. They didn't make the right choice, in my opinion, to protect me then, so how much faith was I supposed to have in them with this?

It was hard watching my parents address this situation, honestly. They wanted to know what I wanted them to do. They assured me they would put him out of the house. My mom wanted to know if I wanted them to call the police and report him. I couldn't take any of it seriously. Honestly, all I could say was, "No, I just want it to stop, again."

He hadn't done anything worse than what my biological father had done to me for years. I was frustrated. She had come to my rescue, but it didn't feel right to me.

As I laid across my bed that night, I felt numb. I couldn't believe she was so ready to react the way a mother should in this situation. However, she couldn't make a better decision when it came to understanding what my father had done to me for years. I couldn't make sense of it. It hurt. Tears streamed down my face and my chest physically ached. My stomach was in knots.

After this incident, I developed a mindset and attitude that aligned with "it is what it is." No one was going to love or protect me the way I felt I should be. I had no allies. I felt like whatever I was going to do from this point on, I was on my own. I was shut in and stuck in a situation where I didn't feel safe.

I remember watching Lifetime movies on TV and seeing other girls who experienced things like me, and their outcomes were different. Each time I watched Lifetime, I developed a new fear that reminded me to keep to myself and mind my manners.

Often, I would do self-pep talks, saying things like, "It's only a short amount of time left before you are free. Just take one day at a time."

Fast forward a few years and prom, graduation, and my first job were upon us.

My first job at a local retail store was a nice escape. It was during my shifts that I was able to meet new people and experience life differently than I had been. I knew it was important that I saved money, and at the same time, I grew a taste for the sales rack and eating out for lunch. The balance was tricky, but I had my goals in place because I still planned to see my exit plan through.

One day, while working, I was approached by a young man who pointed out his friend was interested in me and wanted my number. This was out of the ordinary for me, as I had always been skeptical of people, especially new ones. For some reason, there was an urge in me that nudged me to entertain this notion and I wrote my number on a paper for him to give to his friend.

Within a few days, the friend of the young man who had approached me called my phone. I answered. We talked for a short while on a couple of occasions, and after learning he had been in the military, I felt like I was being set up. I was nervous. I thought there was a good chance he knew my parents and didn't think it was a good idea to participate in any more conversations. I stopped answering his calls for a while.

After some time had passed, he showed up at my job again. We talked and I enjoyed the conversation. Later that day, on my break, I had contacted my mother to coordinate how I would get home that evening. She didn't like driving at night and my father was deployed at the time. She asked if I had anyone who could bring me home. The young man happened to be there and offered to take me home. I remember being very hesitant. My mom seemed to be fine with this. I felt sick to my stomach initially because I didn't really "know" this man and what he was capable of.

At the end of the day, no other takers were available to drive me home, so I walked nervously to his Cadillac and got into the passenger seat. He asked me for the address, and I gave it to him. I was bad with directions and, to be honest, still am to this day.

One false move or turn, brother, and I'm going to roll right out of this moving car, I thought with my hand on the handle of the door.

He was so nice, and I think he sensed my discomfort. He made small talk with me and got me home safe, without incident. He offered to be available to take me home anytime I needed. I thanked him and got out of the car and immediately rushed to the door. I thanked God out loud when I made it to my room.

Before I knew it, he was my "regular" ride home, and the more comfortable I became, the more I loosened my grip on the door handle of his car. Eventually, I didn't even reach for the door handle as I became so comfortable, I was requesting songs to be played on the ride home and laughing effortlessly. We would continue the chat on the phone once I was in the house. I grew to really like being around him.

The more we talked and learned about each other, we realized we had a common interest. We both had a mutual love for music. I wrote poetry and songs, but didn't have any beats or talent in that department. However, he and his best friend were producers and made beats, wrote songs with fire hooks, and recorded them right in the comfort of their home studio! He asked if I would be interested in checking out their studio, and again, I shut down. One, I didn't know what that would look like. Two, my mom would never go for it. So, I dismissed the idea and changed the subject the first few times he extended the offer. I would wrap up the phone calls by telling him I was tired and would go to bed.

On one of our phone calls, he requested to hear my poems. I decided I would share a few with him. He really liked them and shared with me he thought I was talented. He asked me to sing for him and, at first, I was too shy, but advised maybe one day, but it was too soon. He understood and didn't pressure me.

He would play some of his beats for me, which sounded good, but I wasn't able to fully appreciate it due to the phone quality. We laughed and talked about all the things we had experienced earlier in the day before wrapping up the call.

We had some more phone calls, and it usually went the same. One day, we were talking and laughing like we typically did. I remember his voice becoming more serious and he wanted to have a discussion. He started explaining how he had really been enjoying our conversations, he really liked me, and wanted to see where things could go for us. I remember swallowing hard and anticipating what he was going to say next. He took a pause before asking me to be his girlfriend. I took a moment and had to really consider what he was asking. I didn't want a boyfriend at that time, and I was honest with him. I had recently gotten out of a relationship, which wasn't serious, but I wanted to focus on myself. He told me OK, but seemed disappointed with my response. Shortly after, we ended the call amicably. I received a text ten to fifteen minutes later, explaining he needed to pull back as it seemed he liked me more than I liked him. He explained he may not reach out as much due to this reason.

Later that night, I remember running a bath, and while sitting in it, I couldn't stop thinking about him and what he'd said. I got physically sick and the urge to call him back would not let me go. I called him back, and with an attitude, I said, "I will give this a shot, but if it doesn't work, then don't blame me."

It was then official. We were a "thing" and had to embrace what that looked like. We had been talking for some months prior to making it official shortly after I turned eighteen.

Eventually, I was so comfortable talking with him, I was singing and running new ideas by him. I looked forward to his phone calls. He became my sanity in a world that seemed so scrambled. In all my uncertainty, I was sure I valued our friendship and time we spent together.

To celebrate, he took me on our first "date" to O'Charley's and let me order what I wanted. I loved the meal. It was the first real "date" I had ever had, so it was something new for me. Being sheltered my whole life didn't really help me either. I was looking around and still nervous any time we shared or celebrated a "first" for me, anyway.

Prom was just around the corner, so we had those conversations. I didn't know if he would want to go with me or not. He assured me he did. We agreed on a turquoise theme. We didn't have a lot of money, but he sacrificed and made adjustments to show up and make my night special. I really enjoyed the fact that we were able to share this special milestone together.

Next up, was graduation! He was there, cheering me on as I walked the stage. Things moved quickly after this. I was looking at colleges and trying to figure out how I was going to get to and from, as I still didn't have my license at this point.

I decided on a community college that I was going to pay for out of pocket for as long as I could afford it to avoid student loans. I had switched jobs shortly after graduation and was making more money working at a local call center. I had budgeted my funds to ensure I could go full time and still save any little bit I could to try to prep for move-out day.

After a few semesters in college of me paying out of pocket, I felt really good. I wasn't saving as much as I wanted and was paying my parents one hundred dollars a month. My mom came to me and advised that I needed to start paying for an extra class a semester or consider moving out.

After consideration, I decided it would be best if I just saved up a few checks and moved out instead of draining my funds to the max, which would prolong what I wanted to do. I talked it over with my boyfriend and we decided we would move in together, and ultimately, it would save money. I had made the choice to get a one-bedroom apartment and we paid the deposits for the utilities, first month rent and went with fully furnished to start out.

Once I obtained my keys, I went to share the news with my parents. My mom had the talk with me about her feelings on shacking up. I heard her out and ultimately decided I had to do what was best for me, understanding I was responsible for all that came with my decision.

The next part entailed me packing up all my belongings and moving them in to our new home. I was excited and nervous at the same time. I was excited to see my plan come together regarding moving out and creating a life of my own. Yet, I was nervous because I didn't know what the future had in store. I had never lived on my own, but there I was, jumping out into the real world with a man who I had not known a very long time. I didn't let any of that stand in the way of me giving it all I had, though. I went for it, fully committed!

Things between my boyfriend and I were amazing, at first. We rarely disagreed about much. The honeymoon stage was everything! Learning each other, budgeting bills, and embracing every part of our struggle at the same time was exciting.

Things got real for me, at some point. I understood it was different living with someone than seeing them every now and again. When we had our days where we didn't want to be bothered was when it got rough. I realized there weren't many options or places to escape in a one bedroom, one bathroom, 600 square feet apartment. I learned we weren't good at communicating effectively when we were in a bad space mentally, either.

Our age gap was seven years, with him being older than me. I had friends who couldn't understand what we shared in common, and they were vocal about it. When he would go out with his friends, trust wasn't an issue, initially. The real issues started when other people would be in the same space as he and his friends and shared the details of what they witnessed.

At first, I tried to quiet the noise and talk myself out of bringing it up to him. Then, the reports came from credible sources, which got to me. I felt like I was being played. There were instances where people were sending me pictures of him dancing with other women, me seeing text messages pop up on his phone from other women and claims of him being seen in his car with another woman at a gas station when he told me he was working and wouldn't pick up the phone for me.

Trying to talk through these things with him was very painful for me. I always ended up in tears and more confused after the conversation. I would be so mad, the words expressed by me weren't even being received well by him as he would shut down. Many times, the discussions would be one sided because he wouldn't even respond to me. He would start falling asleep in the middle of my rant. This only heightened my frustration, and I had serious trust issues when he wasn't around.

This led me to question everything he told me. I started going through his phone and seeing threads of inappropriate interactions with him and other women. I would then ask him random questions later and when he would lie, so I'd ask to see his phone right on the spot. Sometimes, he would put up a fight and deny me, but other times, he would unlock it, pass it to me, and leave the house. I would become enraged to the point of losing sleep. I constantly brought up these things even when I forgave him. I couldn't let it go.

It seemed like the more I forgave him, the worse things got.

It would get better for the moment, but then slowly, we would work our way up to another situation. No matter how much I would cry, yell, and beg him to do right by me, it seemed like a waste of air. I threatened to leave time after time, but didn't have the strength to see it through. I didn't know where I would go. I didn't want to go back to my parents' house. If I decided to put him out, then where was he going to go? Would he go stay with another woman? Then, what happened if we decided to work it out? Could I take him back? All these questions ran through my mind every time things got heated between us. It kept me stuck. I didn't have any answers that made sense.

I looked to others for guidance but always found myself back to the same solution, which was to stay and suck it up. I prayed and hoped one day he would choose me and change.

He would apologize to me but never had a reason he was doing those things to me. That was the most painful part: not having answers. I never felt secure or safe in our relationship or like I was enough for him.

I was starting to have bad stomach pains and headaches. I was stressed out and had learned I had gallstones. I ended up hitting the floor at work one day, due to the pain I had in my stomach. I would later learn at the hospital that I needed to make a choice to have the gallstones removed or the gallbladder taken out. I confirmed it wasn't an organ that was life threatening if removed and decided to move forward with the surgery. That was a great decision, and life was good for a while after as I didn't experience those unbearable stomach pains that I had also struggled with since early childhood.

Once I healed from that surgery, things were pretty good for a bit. We even entertained the idea of starting our own family. I had been on birth control and was faithful in taking the pills to ensure we didn't have any slip-ups. We were starting to get used to living together and loving each other. We felt like we had reached new heights and milestones in being together, which was great for us. By this time, I had gotten very well acquainted with my then boyfriend and now husband.

There were still some deep, dark secrets I was holding onto that impacted us intimately. I tried to force myself through personal activities. Even with tears streaming down my face, I tried hard. Most times, he wouldn't be able to see my tears because the lights were out, but I struggled in silence again.

One day, he saw my tears and immediately became alarmed. I didn't know what to say. He assured me he supported me and wouldn't force me to do anything I wasn't comfortable with, for whatever reason. It went both ways as I could not enjoy him trying to please me either in that way. It was a mental block for me. I had no desire to try to break down that wall because it would mean I had to go back and recall my past. It hurt so bad to think about those thoughts that I had buried down deep just so I could function. He empathized with me and promised everything was going to be all right.

Experiencing and expressing this painful part of my past helped to put some things in perspective. While things between us were not perfect, the decision to continue to fight for each other was worth it. We made a commitment to try to be better to and for each other.

"Sometimes, the only way to move forward is to acknowledge what happened back then, going back to take a hard look at the foundation you've always believed in. The very foundation you feel has been rock solid until something happens and you're shaken to your core. The life-changing part happens when you realize the very ones who were supposed to protect you failed you in more ways than one. They were so caught up in the image and living the lifestyle they desired, it overshadowed them doing the right thing. It was easier to operate in the lies and manipulation served on a platter as normalcy, which was dressed as dysfunction."

~ Shae Pratcher ~

Chapter 6

Little Man 606

Around nineteen, I remember having pains in my stomach multiple times a week. Some days, the pain was worse than others, but it was uncomfortable, nonetheless. I decided it was time to schedule an appointment with a doctor to confirm what could be contributing to my discomfort. They ran multiple tests, and everything came back normal with my urine and bloodwork. They advised I needed an ultrasound to look into it further. We scheduled it and I waited patiently until that day came.

On the day of the ultrasound, the techs tried to look on the surface but needed to do a pelvic ultrasound. It was the first time, and I was nervous as all get out! The reminder of the unbearable pain I had been experiencing outweighed my fear in that moment, however.

We sat in silence for the most part, but I remember the ultrasound tech stating they were fairly confident they'd found the source of my pain. Minimal information was shared during that visit, but I was advised I would hear from the doctor after they reviewed the ultrasound. I left feeling anxious that day.

What did they see? Was it curable? Was something wrong?

Would they have to take out another organ? Would my body be able to handle another surgery? What would be the side effects of that?

I caught myself spiraling out of control in my mind and needed to... STOP. I prayed to God and decided it was best to just pause all that in my mind until I heard from the doctor.

Within a week, I received a follow-up call and was advised to come in to discuss the details of their observations. Of course, I chose the earliest date they had available.

A couple of days had gone by, and it felt like eternity. I still had to work and function while dealing with the stress that comes with waiting and worrying.

Finally, the day had come! I woke up and got dressed for the follow-up appointment. I arrived early and sat in the parking lot, trying to keep my mind off the "what if" train. I said a long prayer, took a deep breath, and checked in for my appointment. My legs were basically jelly, heart was racing, mind was all over the place and the wait to be called back seemed never ending.

"Ms. Triplett?"

As I grabbed for my purse, I said, "That's me! Yes, I am ready."

The walk to the room was a blur, but the conversation was still one I heard so clearly. The doctor had pictures of the ultrasound to help explain what he needed to break down for me. They explained that the ultrasound showed I had a severe case of what they call PCOS. They went into detail about what it was, saying PCOS was short for Polycystic Ovary Syndrome. He explained there were different levels, but I had many cysts on my ovaries. There were so many, there were risks I needed to consider, prior to deciding how to proceed, then he provided me with a couple options for treatment.

I asked, "What does this impact?"

His response was, "In your case, the ability to have children is the most impacted."

"So, I could never have kids?"

He said, "This is one of the worse cases I've seen in my experience, so yes, it is possible you may never have kids."

Everything else that was discussed during the visit was incomprehensible. His words rolled together and went in one ear and out of the other.

I left feeling very crushed in my spirit. I was lost. I was confused. I tried to think of all the ways this could have happened.

Why is this happening to me? What did I do to deserve all the strife I had experienced until now?

I had a lot to think about. Tears kept streaming down my face as the thoughts continued to pour in. I was in my car alone, having an entire pity party before I knew it. None of the good days I had mattered.

I went home and walked in to share the heartbreaking news with my boyfriend. He listened intently as I sobbed through the details of my appointment. He was calm and had some questions, but not too many. He tried his best to assure me that everything was going to be OK but I didn't feel much better.

Over the next few days, I called family and friends to share the news. I cried so much, I was mentally depleted.

Since a young child, one of my biggest dreams had always been to have kids. *Did God really create me without including kids in the plan for my life?* I couldn't make sense of it. I couldn't just accept that.

Over the next few months, I found myself drowning in research about PCOS and treatment options. I read countless scenarios of different women who had severe cases of PCOS and how they prevailed. There were so many outcomes, I think I was worse off mentally than I was when I found out about the diagnosis. I tried to calm down and talk myself off the ledge by remembering all the positive Bible verses that had been shared with me over the years. I wanted to be OK. I wanted to not stress or worry about it. At the end of the day, the fact was, I knew I wanted kids, and knowing there was a possibility I could be robbed of that opportunity didn't sit right with me. I was hurt. I was disappointed. I was angry.

Over the next two to three months, I looked at alternate fertility treatments. In my mind, nothing was off the table. I wanted to understand the risks and had already told myself it was worth it. I had even looked at the adoption process in case this option had failed and told myself that maybe that was what God wanted for me.

Once I had my plan A, B, C, and D in place, I circled back to discuss it with my boyfriend. He listened with such patience before telling me to stop. He expressed how much he loved me and needed me to understand that even if we could not have kids together, he would love me, anyway. He assured me it wasn't going to be something that would make or break our relationship. He told me to not believe what the doctors said.

"Just because that's what they told you or what they have seen in their experience, doesn't mean it'll be yours."

I wasn't so sure. I didn't believe it. It wasn't even about that to me. I was more upset there was a big possibility I would never be able to have kids. Tears streamed down my face again. I sat and stared blankly through him as he tried to console me. I was empty. I decided to let this subject rest because it was upsetting me to the point of no return.

I was still bothered by the diagnosis over the next few months. I decided to get off my birth control because, in my mind, there wasn't a point since I couldn't have kids, anyway. I continued to research in silence about what other women did to cope with the diagnosis. I saw so many stories and so many different outcomes. I wanted to be hopeful.

One day, I came across some information that really changed the course of my life. There were articles and details about the importance of understanding your body as a woman. I had learned about ovulation tracking. What a gem I had found on that day!

For the next few weeks, I was in research overload, and I wanted to know everything there was about ovulation tracking! I started going to the stores and buying so many ovulation and pregnancy tests.

I decided I would try to be patient with the process, but wasn't against giving it a push. So, I talked to my boyfriend and explained that I understood things had been crazy, and I was willing to try to see if I could get pregnant prior to escalating to the other options we had discussed. He agreed to work together and be patient with me as I entertained this approach. Little did we know, this decision would only intensify our relationship on a whole new level!

When I used the ovulation strips in the morning, it would set the tone for my entire day. For a couple months, it was negative every. Single. Day. *Was this normal? Was I using the strips correctly? Did I have other issues the doctors could not see? Did I need to schedule a follow up?*

Months of disappointment, letdowns, and being crushed in spirit felt as if I was repeatedly ripping the band aid off an open wound. I couldn't heal. I didn't feel better. I was over it. I didn't know what to think, believe, or anything.

And then a shift happened. It was a morning I could never forget. I got up and followed the same routine, expecting the same results. As I dipped the ovulation test strip and laid it flat to wait on the results, something felt different. I got up, washed my hands, and peered at the strip as it had generated results I had never seen before. There were two lines on the test strip, and I was overjoyed and overtaken by emotions! I was so happy, all I could do was smile and call my boyfriend and let him know. He wanted to know what this meant, and I let him know we needed to "do it"! As a matter of fact, we needed to do it for at least the next three to four days straight to make sure the sperm was there.

All day long, all I could think about was making sure we had sex, so our possibility of conceiving was higher. Later that evening, as exhausted as we both were, the adrenaline was pumping, and we did it! I was happy and hopeful for the first time in almost a year. Things were good. Maybe there was still a chance kids were in the cards for us.

The next couple of days were about the same. We knew what we had to do, and we did it! We patiently waited the next month to see if I would come on my cycle, and I did. I was disappointed, but thought back on how happy I was to know that at least my body could ovulate. I was trying to count my wins.

The next few months went about the same way. We were overly excited when the ovulation test would show up positive. We would prep ourselves to have sex and wait patiently to see how the next month would turn out for us.

We began getting used to the disappointment, month over month. I reverted to being depressed and things got rough. I was so worried about the ovulation process that, along the way, we lost the "fun" in it, and it began feeling like a chore. There were nights where we couldn't even enjoy it because it felt forced.

I remember afterward, instead of cuddling, I would prop my legs up on the wall to be sure the sperm was staying inside of me long enough without dripping out. This got old, and we were holding it in versus being honest with each other, which spilled over into other areas of our relationship. We started resenting each other without even knowing it. It wasn't until we started arguing about the smallest things and realizing how things would blow up that we acknowledged it was problematic. We needed to take a time out and that was what happened.

Things hit the fan and there was no other way to deal with it but head on. We were both exhausted. We had spent so much time and energy on this one aspect of our life, we started losing each other along the way. Things were crazy. I felt crazy, like nothing else mattered. Looking back, there was so much money, effort, and time spent and we couldn't get any of it back. We had to be honest with each other and decided it was best to take a break from focusing on "having a baby."

I was not happy, but I understood and agreed. In the moment, I felt defeated again. All the things we had worked for and toward had been put on pause once more.

Before I knew it, I was twenty years old. A whole year later, and I felt like there were still no answers. However, our relationship was in a much better place. We had found ways to cope with what "was" and learned to deal with it better than before. I grew comfortable in understanding that what will be, will be, and staying in the place of contentment was best for my mental health and the relationship. I still cried in the shower sometimes. I embraced the car rides alone so I could really acknowledge the true feelings I had.

Another five months passed, and I was finally in a better place and space in my life. I was honestly getting used to life as it was. One day, during this time period, we decided to go and hang out with some friends. We were so excited about it. We got there and laughed, danced, and ate good! I wasn't a drinker, but occasionally, during social events, I would. I had a Mike's Hard Lemonade, and it went down smooth, then I felt less intense. We laughed some more and talked about old times before deciding it was time for us to head back home.

Just as we gave our hugs and headed down their driveway to the car, I felt an overwhelming urge of sickness come over me. It was so sudden, I remember throwing up right in their driveway. I was slightly embarrassed but not surprised because I wasn't a drinker and knew I'd had a couple, which was more than I could handle.

We drove home and I just wanted to lie down. I remember getting up in a panic and grabbing my phone to see what day of the month it was. I quickly started trying to recollect when I had my menstrual cycle last.

Just for a peace of mind, we decided to drive to Walmart and get a pregnancy test after frantically looking under the sink for any left over from before. We were able to get a pack with two in it and drive back home. The whole time, I remember telling myself how I couldn't afford to let myself get overly excited or too wrapped up in my thoughts of what I wanted. I gave myself a pep talk before I took the test to try to keep my crazy in check.

I took the test and washed my hands. I still wasn't feeling my best, so I sat on the toilet seat cover with my hand on my head, waiting for the results. My stomach was in knots, torn between what I wanted and what the reality would be. Reminders of the pain I had felt for the past sixteen months rang loud in my ear. Just as my eyes filled with tears, I looked at the test strip and, to my surprise, it had two lines! One of the lines was so faint, I seriously thought my eyes were playing tricks on me! I got my flashlight and wiped my eyes at least ten times before running to share the news with my boyfriend. I was truly overwhelmed with what I saw. I couldn't believe the test had come up positive! How? Really? Was I dreaming?

I started to cry and pinch myself over and over again. I remember thinking if I'm dreaming, please let me live in this moment forever. He was so happy, and we celebrated and in that same moment I got sad. I became nervous.

I said, "Oh my goodness, I was drinking! What if something is wrong? What if I harmed the baby? What am I supposed to do next? I need to schedule a doctor's appointment ASAP to get checked."

He tried to calm me down and once again assure me that everything was going to be all right. He said we just needed to take it one step at a time. I took a deep breath and decided I needed to lie down for the night and deal with everything over the next few days.

I woke up in the morning and immediately pinched myself to see if I was dreaming. Then, went to look at the pregnancy test again to make sure it was still "positive." I took another test just to make sure and it was positive again! I smiled to myself and kept thanking God repeatedly! I started making calls to the doctor office to see what I needed to do. They asked all these questions I should've known the answer to, and had it been about six months back, I would've, but I didn't. I wasn't sure how far I was or when my last menstrual period was because I was trying to be less stressed and let things happen naturally if it was meant to be. They made the appointment and was sure to advise me of the real possibility of it being a false "positive" and waiting until they checked again before taking it as a confirmed pregnancy. I got off the call yet again, feeling knocked down. *What if it is a false positive?*

I got lost in my thoughts, thinking what if I couldn't give him any kids? Although he would say it's not a deal breaker, I had to be real with myself, and I often wondered if he would see me as less of a woman one day because I wasn't able to give him any kids. What if he did feel strongly about wanting more than the two kids he already had? What does that look like for us? All these things were real to me because this was someone I felt I wanted to spend the rest of my life with. The rollercoaster ride was unnerving and becoming uncomfortable and unbearable the longer we stayed on. I felt like I was unstable with my thoughts, feelings, and actions at times because of this void that weighed so heavily on my heart.

How do I not internalize these things? How do I process it the right way? How will this impact us now that we have gotten to this level if things fall through again? Can my heart handle another heartbreak?

The day came and I showed up, ready for whatever at my doctor's appointment. They did another pregnancy test, and it came up positive, but they also drew blood and confirmed we were pregnant! I was so happy, and I remember asking how it was possible with my severe case of PCOS. They advised they were doctors and could only provide information based on what the diagnosis was, but things change in time and these kinds of things happen sometimes. I was just happy to know I could get out of my head and move forward with the best news I had received up to this point in my life! We discussed what happened during pregnancy, the appointments, and what to expect.

Due to the timing of my pregnancy, I was on Tricare for part of my pregnancy and TennCare for the remaining. In the early stages, all the appointments were fine. The doctors and nurses were all nice.

I was enjoying being pregnant and the experience was breathtaking at times. I was finally able to go through this with someone I was in love with and have my biggest dream come true. I was on top of the world. No other feeling in the world compared to the unspeakable joy I had. It was happening for me... for us... and I was so blessed to be pregnant with our first baby boy!

I had more ultrasounds than the average pregnant woman, and about halfway through, they noticed our son's kidney was enlarged, so they referred us to see a specialist in Nashville. We made that drive so many times, I could drive there without directions if I had to.

During the many visits, we were so happy to see our little man and get the ultrasound pictures. We would smile and look through them very often as we made our way back to Clarksville, TN, on a weekly basis. Toward the end of the pregnancy, the doctors decided it would be best to have him in Nashville just to make sure if there was any care necessary for his enlarged kidney, he would have the staff readily available. We understood and agreed.

I remember asking questions to make sure the kidney concern wasn't life threatening and they assured me it was not. I was able to relax knowing he would come into this world with some of the best doctors available to him, should he need it for his kidneys.

During the last round of ultrasound pictures, I noticed it looked like our son had six fingers. I pointed it out to my mother and boyfriend, but they said no. At the last ultrasound, I asked the tech, "I'm not trying to be funny, but does it look like he has six fingers to you?"

She replied, "Let me see."

Sure enough, when she checked, she confirmed it did look that way to her. She went out of the room and spoke with someone but came back in and assured me this was something that could happen sometimes and it was no big deal. It was usually a painless procedure that could be done at birth to remove the extra finger. We had someone in our family who had six fingers and it had been removed before, so this wasn't alarming to me. They again assured us that everything looked fine and confirmed our date to be induced for the delivery would be May 28, 2009.

I woke up, ready to meet our little man on May 28, 2009. We drove to Nashville and got checked in. I was in labor for about twenty-three hours before they decided to finally extend the offer of a c-section to me. I gladly took it as I was ready to meet our little man, and also ready to eat.

They prepped me, and on May 29, 2009, at 6:06 p.m., we welcomed our first baby boy, Braylen Makai Pratcher, into the world! He was seven pounds, six and a half ounces When I woke up, I was in another room and did not see my baby initially. I remember feeling disconnected and discombobulated.

I asked my mom, "Was everything OK? Did I have a baby?"

She answered yes to both questions.

I wanted to see my baby. The nurses finally came in and advised they would be able to take me to see him after a while, due to my c-section. They had to get me to where I could get up and walk so I could be transported to the NICU where our baby boy was.

Prior to me making my way to see him, the doctor came in to talk with us. He advised they had run some tests and were running a few more as it appeared our son may have a chromosome disorder, but they were waiting on a few more results to confirm. He recommended I try to walk so I could get to see him sooner than later.

Within a few hours, the doctors came back in and confirmed my worst nightmare. He told us Braylen had Trisomy 13, which is a fatal chromosome disorder. Typically, most babies only live a couple of days. He encouraged us to spend as much time as possible with him. My world shattered.

The moment that was supposed to be the happiest day of my life was snatched from me. My first reaction was to break down crying, but the pain from my c-section reminded me I couldn't do that.

There I was, in the hospital bed, stifling my cries due to the physical pain of my cut. My heart was so heavy. I finally pushed myself to get up out of the bed and walk so I could get to my baby.

I remember sitting in the NICU with my head cocked to the side, staring at him. He was so perfect to me. He had six fingers and six toes on both hands and feet. He had the prettiest shade of brown hair I'd ever seen. His skin tone and texture were just perfect. I couldn't see him the way they saw him. I didn't believe he was "sick." He looked so perfect to me. He had the softest cry I'd ever heard to this day. I rubbed his feet and each one of his toes. I held his hand with tears streaming down my face, feeling so helpless and hopeless, but trying to hold it together for him.

I wanted him to be the miracle. I believed God could do it! I wanted God to do it! He was so healthy in size. How could there be anything wrong? I didn't want to accept it. It was so hard to leave him and go back to my room. I was truly empty. I felt abandoned. My heart had been shattered in the worse way. In my mind, there was no coming back from this. I needed to do some research to see if there were miracles. I needed to know for myself that this was a real thing, and it was fatal. I was dying on the inside, worried that I would wake up and he would be gone, and I wouldn't have a chance to say goodbye. That became my new fear that clung to me.

The doctors came in and explained that he had lived a few days, and when it was time for me to be released, we had a decision to make. He could be released to a hospice there as he had to be tube fed because he could not suck, breathe and swallow simultaneously. We had to fill out paperwork to decide whether we wanted them to resuscitate him repeatedly should he stop breathing. They explained the effects of doing this. We had to leave him at the hospice and drive from Nashville, TN, to Clarksville, TN, multiple times a week. We were exhausted, but it was the only way. I needed help as I was healing and the staff at the hospice were on call for our son and not me. Once I healed enough, I moved in with my son at the hospice.

Braylen lived twenty-eight wonderful days. During this time, we took plenty of pictures, embraced every moment and dedicated him back to the Lord. I remember waking up with him in my arms the day he passed, and he was staring at me with one eye fully open, and the other eye half closed. There was a peace that came over me and it felt as if he was telling me so much in those moments without saying anything.

About an hour and a half later, the nurse came to advise me he had been having back-to-back seizures all morning. Shortly after her saying this, he went back to having them, but they lasted longer than before. He went into one and I had a decision to make to prevent him from being in pain or swallowing his tongue. I chose to allow them to give him a shot to make him comfortable, and we held him until he took his last breath. When he took his last breath and changed colors, I remember feeling like all the breath in my body left and I hit the floor. I wasn't ready.

I remember hearing my mom screaming, asking God to please keep me, and then a new reality hit me. My worse fear was here, and I had to deal with it. I took a deep breath, said a prayer, and stood up. Braylen started breathing, but he never opened his eyes again. I held him for a couple of hours until he finally took his final breath. I strongly believe that God allowed Braylen to start breathing the second time to give us an opportunity to cope with what was happening. Braylen went home to be with the Lord on June 26, 2009.

-I remember feeling lost.
-I was hurt.
-I felt hopeless.
-I was angry.
-I was upset.
-I was disappointed.
-I felt my life was OVER.

Even with all these emotions running high, we still had even more difficult decisions to make in the coming days. Do we have a funeral? Where do we bury him? Do we cremate him? How do we keep him close in our hearts and minds? What do we do to keep his memory alive?

We chose to have him cremated because it gave us the opportunity to bring him home, which was something we could not do up to that point. We wanted a chance to spread his ashes one day with future kids after sharing his story, if God saw fit to bless us with another opportunity. It was our way of holding on to hope, believing it could or would help us heal. We believed it was not the end.

Within seven days of having his ceremony to celebrate his life, I had to go back to work. Bills were still due. My pain was still so raw and real, however. I remember screaming, crying, gathering myself and going back into work and acting like everything was OK. I felt alone, like no one got it. I wanted to go be with my son. I felt there was no way I would live past this moment.

Things would happen just when I started to cope with the reality of our son being gone. Someone at work would ask how my son was, and at first, I was understanding that maybe they didn't know, and I would smile through the tears while speaking softly, letting them know he had passed, unfortunately.

As the weeks and months went by, though, it hurt even more. I didn't feel like time was healing my wounds. I felt like I was getting worse. Then, people still asked about our son, and I got angry. I would have outbursts and shout he was dead with no further explanation, before walking off.

I couldn't worry about anybody else and their hurt feelings anymore because I was living it and they weren't. They had no idea how many people had asked me the same question and how painful it was to keep reliving it. I couldn't talk about it at home because I was scared I would trigger my husband into having a moment and was unsure what he would do.

At one point, there was awesome support, and I could always reach out to family or friends. Then, there were times in the wee hours of the night that no one was available. Even when some people were available, the advice wasn't helpful and ended up being more damaging. While understanding not everyone had the right words to say, it was awful to hear some of the things people said. I'd been told to let it go and had someone say he couldn't even rest in peace because I kept reliving what happened. I realized it was just me and my thoughts. This pain was heavy and it was not letting up.

It got me down so bad one day, I thought it was worth it to end it all. All my pain, suffering, and heartache. I still had the pain pills in my cabinet from my c-section. I had my mind set that I was going to take every one of them and whatever happened… happened.

As I walked down the stairs and through my living room, my knees grew very weak. I let out a cry from deep within and I told God, "If You don't come and see about me now, I'm not going to make it!"

The tears were flowing, and my heart was racing. My head was spinning and hurting at the same time. Before I knew it, my knees were on the floor just before the entryway between my living room and kitchen. I felt the most calming feeling pass over me, and it was a peace that surpasses all understanding. In that moment, I knew God loved me. I knew He cared. I knew He was going to bring me out on the other side better if I didn't quit. I was assured in that moment that HE was there and has never and would never leave me nor forsake me!

IT WASN'T UNTIL I REALLY LET GO AND LET GOD WORK IN, ON, and through me that I was able to be free. Free from myself. Free from the feelings. Free from the lies of the enemy. Free from living and feeling "stuck". I started to really LIVE.

I started reading my Bible, going to church, and surrounding myself with positive people constantly. I had to learn how to go back to the basics, which was my foundation in Christ for the comfort and love that was needed to carry me through. It wasn't easy and it felt like a long process.

God used me even in my brokenness to be an outreach for other young women who had loss babies, almost immediately after I lost my son. I remember asking God, "How am I going to help them when I don't even feel like I can help myself? How can I help someone else when I haven't healed?"

BUT GOD DID IT! He used me to help others and he healed me in the process!

The AMAZING blessing is that because I didn't quit and stayed faithful, God has blessed us with three more kids! I am constantly reminded of His covering and that when God says YES, it's blessed! We still feel Braylen's presence, and whenever we see the number 6:06, we know he is still with us! We say, "We love you, Braylen," in sync as a way to keep his memory alive. We celebrate his birthday milestones together as well. I understand that no other kids can replace him, and his memory is forever engraved in and on our hearts and minds.

Chapter 7
Breakdown To Breakthrough

In the wake of trying to process and recover from the loss of our first-born son, my mind was racing. I couldn't help but wonder what was next for me. I remember thinking my life was spiraling out of control again. I wanted to get a grip and feel like I had some sense of control, but I really struggled with it. Things were foggy.

A few months after celebrating the twenty-eight days of life for our firstborn, another shift happened. I decided I would have a drink. Shortly after the chat with a friend as I headed home, I felt a wave of sickness out of nowhere. I had to pull over, it was so strong. I threw up on the side of the road. Then, it was followed by a headache I couldn't shake.

Over the next couple of days, I thought about when my last menstrual was and realized I was late. I immediately became stressed. I felt like I was going crazy because I didn't want to feel any more pain. I waited a few days to see if my cycle would show up, and when it did not, I decided to take a pregnancy test. As I was going through the very familiar process, I tried to have a pep talk with myself to keep from losing it.

"No matter what happens or what the results are, you got this! What's supposed to be will be."

I washed my hands and walked out of the bathroom to give it time to process. When I came back in and glanced at the test, I saw only one line. My heart skipped a beat, and although we weren't trying to conceive, I was disappointed. I slid the test off the counter and into the trash quickly in frustration. Tears streamed down my face, and I told God I was tired of this. Tired of being let down. Tired of feeling like I have nothing to look forward to.

I went in the living room and listened to some music to try to deal with my emotions. When my boyfriend came home, he quickly recognized something was bothering me. I tried to shake it off and act like it was nothing. I struggled to put into words what I wanted to say, so I went back to the bathroom to retrieve the pregnancy test from the trash can. When I got it out of the trash can and looked closer, the results had changed. I saw the same strong line, but then a very faint second line! I couldn't believe it! I wanted to, but I was like, no way!

I stammered over my words at this point, trying to explain what had happened. I asked him to confirm what he saw as I didn't trust myself in that moment. He confirmed he saw two lines, with one being very faint. Before I knew it, tears flowed uncontrollably, and I didn't know how to feel.

I spent the next few days in disbelief that I was pregnant again. I scheduled a doctor's appointment and tried to remain as stress free as I could. Due to being high risk, I was scheduled for the earliest appointment available.

I arrived for my ultrasound appointment and the pregnancy was confirmed. The tech didn't talk much, which led me to believe something was wrong. She finished up and advised the doctor would be in touch.

A few days later, I heard from the doctor, and they wanted me to come in to discuss the results. Once in the office, the doctor explained that during any pregnancy, there were certain things they looked for in order to confirm it was a viable pregnancy. They explained I had a couple of the things, but the fetal pole was not detected, which led them to believe this may not be a viable pregnancy.

About three months into the pregnancy, I became more hopeful. That was until I felt a rush of fluids come out as I sat at my desk at work. I immediately panicked. I made it to the bathroom to discover I had started bleeding and it had gone through my pants. I had a jacket and had to wrap it around my waist to spare myself the embarrassment. Additionally, I had to find someone who could take me to the ER immediately. I had a good friend who agreed to leave work and drive my car to the ER.

Once I arrived, there seemed to have been no urgency from the staff, understanding I was high risk. They let me sit in the wheelchair, bleeding through my clothes, for what seemed like hours. I was so over it, all I could do was cry.

At some point, I went back up to the window and explained I needed to be seen right away as I had just loss a baby I had carried full term a few months back. I expressed it seemed I was losing another baby in that moment and I wasn't doing OK.

They eventually took me back and confirmed I had indeed miscarried. They recommended I allow the process to run its course and follow up with my primary doctor.

Another devastating day in the books for me. I was very sad. I felt let down by God again. I was very broken, and this became a dark period for me. I barely had any words to speak. I couldn't describe how numb I was. I didn't want the apologies, empathy, or sympathy. I honestly just wanted to not feel all the emotions I had going through me, day in and day out.

I felt the doctors were right. Maybe I couldn't have kids and it wasn't in the cards for me. I got to where I didn't want to have any kids. At least that was what I told myself to shield myself from the pain.

I got rid of all the ovulation and pregnancy tests. I had resorted to living my life expecting I was meant to be barren. My womb did not prove to be fruitful in a way I would have hoped. While I didn't find peace or happiness in this, I had to accept that was my truth. I could only go off my previous experience, but little did I know, God had different plans for me.

Just as I gave up the idea of having kids, the following year, God showed up and showed out! I became pregnant again and gave birth to our healthy baby boy. We named our rainbow baby Jaylen Andre' Tyrik Pratcher!

We decided to push forward from being engaged to tying the knot and making it official four months after having Jaylen!

About fourteen months of pure joy, dirty diapers, snotty noses among all the milestones in between, there came another surprise. I remember being sick and nauseous, took a pregnancy test, and yet again... I was pregnant! This time, I cried, but my tears were not easily identified as being connected with joy. I didn't know how I went from being "infertile" to "fertile myrtle" and my mind couldn't wrap around it easily.

We had full-time bills that were already accounted for before the checks were deposited and were just adjusting to having a one-year-old. The fact that he was still in diapers, and we would have to adjust to a newborn, meant more money on diapers, which made it real for me. I cried hysterically because I did not see a logical way that we would be able to adjust financially or mentally.

I made the doctor's appointment to confirm we were indeed pregnant again. We scheduled the additional appointments because I was high risk, due to my history. I became stressed immediately because I knew this would require triple the doctor's appointments out of town and trying to figure out how we were going to accomplish this seemed unreal.

We had one reliable vehicle and both of us were working and had to get Jaylen to daycare each morning. This was a struggle we had not yet mastered. However, we agreed that if God would bring us to it, then He would bring us through it and we moved in that Spirit.

My mind was at ease as much as one could expect. I was working at Walmart, unloading trucks, when I found out I was pregnant. I knew I needed to get an accommodation to move to a less strenuous position to ensure the safety of our unborn child. It seemed like trying to get this accomplished was a struggle, so I had to make do until they could make the arrangements.

One day, while working, I went to the restroom to discover I was bleeding. Immediately, I became numb, and panic-stricken. Tears welled up in my eyes and I called my husband so we could go to the ER. It seemed like when you were experiencing these kinds of devastating moments, no one around you had a sense of urgency.

By the time I was seen, they did a pelvic ultrasound and told me the doctor would be in to talk to me shortly. I was emotionless. I tried to remain hopeful, but the amount of blood I had seen wouldn't allow me to be naive. Once again, I tried to have a pep talk with myself so I wouldn't respond irrationally. My husband rubbed on me and said all the right things. He assured me, no matter what, we would be OK. He grew quieter as we patiently waited for them to come back with an update.

The doctor came in and pulled up a seat. I was convinced my heart stopped for a moment before finding its beat again, which felt like it was going to jump through my throat. The doctor explained they had identified it as a threatened miscarriage, due to the baby detaching from my uterus. He advised me of my options to take a pill that would force the remaining pregnancy tissue out of my body or to let the process happen naturally. I declined to take the pill as I had already experienced miscarriages and my body processed everything fine. The cramps were nerve-racking, and I was sad. He explained to me I needed to follow up with my primary care doctor the next week to ensure everything passed through like it was supposed to. If not, they would have to complete a D&C. I acknowledged what he said with a head nod with the remaining energy I had.

They got me the discharge paperwork that showed the diagnosis with the threatened miscarriage details, and I folded them and was wheeled down to the exit. I stared blankly with no emotion and waited for my husband to pull the car up. He helped me in the car, and I remember laying my head up against the window on the passenger side, tears flowing down my face silently all the way home.

I didn't want to talk. I couldn't feel anything. However, I still had a baby at home who needed me to pull it together. I took a few hours and tried to process what was happening. I finally made a few calls. People said what they felt I wanted to hear but, in all honesty, nothing made me feel better.

Then, I remember calling my little brother and explaining to him what had happened. He listened to everything I said and didn't interrupt me. Then he said to me, "I understand all of that, sis, but you don't know what God can do."

I advised him, "I understand that, but I have experienced miscarriages in the past and knew what it felt like and this was definitely it. They also did the pelvic ultrasound and saw the baby had already detached and everything was clearing my uterus."

He told me, "OK, but man has been wrong before. They told you you would never have kids, remember? What happened? You have had two kids, although one is in heaven. So, just try to take it easy and go to the doctor like you supposed to and see what happens from there." I took in what he said. "I'm always here for you, sis. You know you can call me whenever you need to."

He had no idea he had just breathed life back into me, even though the odds were stacked against me. I cried that night like a big baby who had lost their best friend.

I woke up the next day and prayed to God, asking Him for a miracle. I told Him, ultimately, it's Your will that will be done. I want to see Your power and I believe YOU have the final say.

Inside, I still felt empty, but all I could do was let the process run its course. I enjoyed my husband and our baby boy over the next few days leading up to my follow up appointment.

I went in for the follow-up appointment and remembered feeling the same rush of emotions I felt some years back. It was just shortly after I lose my first born that I went in for the postpartum checkup and everyone had their newborn babies but me. I tried to sit there and think of all the positive scriptures I had hidden in my heart. I tried to speak Jeremiah 29:11 over myself. The tears came and flowed like a river.

I grabbed my purse and rushed to the window, asking to be rescued back then, and once again, I begged for the same request on that day. I was overwhelmed with my emotions that a person, let alone, I could take so many losses and be expected to be OK. I wasn't OK. I was breaking down and it was starting to show. They were very apologetic and offered to pull me back into the room until the ultrasound tech was available to check me for the follow up to the threatened miscarriage.

It felt like at least an hour had passed. I was alone in this room with just me and my thoughts. I didn't know what I was supposed to feel or think. I had been through this before, though, so I knew what to expect. I just wanted it to be over with so I could go back home and start the healing process and get back to my life. It was in that moment they finally swung the door open and welcomed me back.

As I got undressed from the waist down and laid up on the table, tears streamed down my face very slowly. The ultrasound tech came back in the office and made small talk with me. We talked briefly about what had happened that led me back here to the follow-up appointment. Through many tears, I choked over my words, but explained I started bleeding heavily and went to the ER. They checked me and confirmed I was in the middle of miscarrying and had given me my options and told me to follow up just to make sure everything cleared.

She started checking me out. She had turned the screen so that only she could see what was on it. I stopped talking and desperately waited for her to tell me anything. After what seemed like twenty minutes of silence, she said, "Oh my God, there's a heartbeat."

My head popped up off the table and I asked her to repeat what she said. She turned the volume up and what I heard blessed my LIFE! It was my baby's heartbeat! I could not believe it. She went out to grab the doctor to pull the file and confirm what was documented by the ER. She explained to me that the baby was in there with a strong heartbeat! I was crying now, but for a very different reason than I was initially! All I could do was cry and keep saying, "Thank You, God. There is nothing my God can't do! Praise will forever be on my lips!"

She confirmed everything looked good and that we would have some additional follow-ups to ensure everything continued to look fine. As she left the room, I could not keep from smiling and thanking God! My entire life changed on this DAY! I knew God was real and that he had done it AGAIN for us!

I heard the Spirit say, "Double for your trouble." I didn't know how we were going to do it, but I knew that what was meant to be, would be. Life would find a way.

As I continued the pregnancy, I tried not to stress. Hubby and I had hit a rough patch in our marriage. There were a lot of stressful things that happened, and he entertained conversations with other women. I remember going through his phone a few times while I was pregnant, and each time, I found some woman he was messaging. It made me very upset and caused us to argue more times than I liked to remember.

The sacrifices I made felt unnoticed, which made me feel unappreciated. It was a stressful time for me as I was carrying another baby and he had a total disregard, it seemed, for what we had experienced. I became distraught and withdrew emotionally from our partnership. I was crying often and had made it clear I was unhappy. I explained that every time I got pregnant, it seemed like he stepped out or checked out of our marriage and it was very hard to accept and understand. There were never valid reasons as to why he would do it that made me feel comfortable.

I decided I would seek a divorce lawyer because I was tired of dealing with the disrespect. I advised him the real problem here was not that I questioned his love for me, but he didn't respect me enough to stay committed to me. In my opinion, he had no integrity. It was hurtful. I was scared that God would punish us both due to his indiscretions. I remember praying very intentionally and often to God to not punish me due to his choices. I assured God that I had what it takes and would do whatever to ensure I give thanks for my many blessings. I begged God to please not allow anything to happen to my children.

Shortly after I gave birth to our daughter, Janiyah, things changed. We shifted for the moment, but I had grown a dislike for the things that had happened. I had no more patience.

I left Walmart and started working at Agero. I had made my mind up I would give this job everything I could to ensure I grew and learned as much as they would allow. Life was good.

Then, a few months in, another incident happened between my husband and a woman at his job. That was it. My breaking point. I was done having the same conversations repeatedly, crying, and trying to over-explain my worth that he clearly didn't see or appreciate. I prayed to God, but didn't wait around for any answer or clarity.

I went to the store and purchased every moving box they had on the shelf. I came home and packed everything I and our kids owned and decided to go back to my parents' house. Back to the same bedroom I had slept in as a teenager, except now with two kids. I left all the furniture and everything else and couldn't worry about it because I wanted to be free from the chaos. I had a lot to think about. I had some important decisions to make. I was not happy because I found myself in a tight place on high alert, but felt this was as good as it could get at the time.

My kids and I had to adjust to being in a different environment. I planned for the kids to visit with him and spend time. I made so many trips back and forth, but for my peace of mind, it was worth it.

After some time had passed, I had to decide what was the best next step for me. I sat down with my grandmother and had a real heart to heart. She put a lot of things in perspective for me to help me make a solid decision. Her support was made known, and she provided me with her wisdom and knowledge that I carried with me from that moment on.

"No one is perfect," she began. "Your grandfather and I had many trials and tests that we've had to overcome during the years, and we did so together. We understood that we were two human beings, who were flawed, so if you're expecting perfection, you'll always be let down, and so will your partner," she schooled.

I was all ears as she fed my spirit with her words of encouragement.

Continuing, she said, "In life, we must understand that what we don't go through with one person, we might just go through with someone else. And I want you to take a hard look at what you and your husband are currently facing and think about the pros and cons. I want you to think about those babies of yours, too, because while it's possible for someone else to love them, nobody will love them like the two of you."

"I'm not telling you what to do one way or another, but if things were that bad in your marriage, we would never convince you to stay. But I want you to really think things through and take your time doing so. You don't want to make a permanent decision based on temporary emotions."

I heard her loud and clear and knew I had a lot to think about.

"One thing I know to be true is that your husband loves you and I see it in his eyes. But even those who love us can make poor choices, and you're not exempt from that. We all need a little grace sometimes, especially in marriage because it takes real effort."

My grandmother left me with these parting words. "It's not about being right but it's about considering all things and being careful of what stick we use to measure others' flaws as we should expect to be measured with the same." She wiped my tears from my face.

"The decision to stay or leave is ultimately a choice you have to make, and I don't need to know your choice one way or another. However, I recommend making a choice when you've had some time to think and talk it over with God. I do believe your marriage can work if you both are willing to put in the work. We are all people and operate in the flesh, trying to come together as one, which is a challenge in itself." She hugged me and we shared I love yous, and I thanked her for her wisdom and kind words to me.

It changed the dynamic of my marriage. It helped me be more conscious of my expectations of not just my husband, but of people. I needed a reminder that we were all human and fall short and need grace extended to us. Also, just because people don't think the way I do or decide to do something I wouldn't doesn't mean they don't love me or are bad people. We all have flaws and fall short differently. It's OK to be disappointed and express that, but equally important to weigh the severity of the situation, prior to making a decision regarding the way ahead.

My husband had been reaching out to me to try to make things right. He sent multiple messages, apologizing and trying to explain that he knew he had messed up. He sent me a song that he had written and produced that was dedicated to me, acknowledging his mistakes and expressing his love for me. I listened to the song and appreciated his effort. I couldn't just accept him back, though, because I needed him to take our marriage serious. I really needed time to let what my grandmother said soak in before I made a decision as well. He understood and respected my wishes.

A bit more time had passed, and he was dedicated to the cause of showing me he had time to think while we were apart, and he knew where he wanted to be was with his family. He planned a family trip to the zoo, and I agreed to go with him so we could talk through it. During this trip, I was able to express my stance on the way things had been up to that point.

I also explained that while I didn't expect him to be perfect, I expected he would respect me the way I did him. I didn't entertain men because I made a vow to him before God. I told him I didn't want him to feel forced to be with me because we had kids together or because it was convenient. I explained he should know I didn't want him to be anywhere he didn't want to be.

We needed to make a commitment to each other to love and respect each other enough to be straight up if we realized we were no longer happy with our circumstances. We agreed. He assured me I wouldn't regret working through our problems together. I told him to let me think about it for a little while longer.

I prayed to God, asking for clear guidance on what to do. I cried and told Him exactly how I felt and expressed I wanted my marriage to work, but only if He blessed it. The next few days were good. I decided to work on a transition to going back home so my family could be together. He was happy and I was hopeful.

Some months had passed, and we were doing better. Although my heart still ached when I thought about some of the text messages I had seen, I tried not to bring it up because I felt guilty. If I forgave him, was it fair for me to still harbor ill feelings and bring it up?

The decision to come back was like a peace offering and I wanted to do my part, but it was hard. That was my truth. There were many nights I ran the shower and locked the bathroom door so I could cry in peace. I felt like I was forced to suffer in silence again as I had done as a child. I remember thinking I was cursed and wasn't worthy of true happiness. I had convinced myself that if my biological father could do what he did to me, no other man would respect or love me. I started questioning if I should even have expectations of people at all.

It hurt me deeper because my husband knew my fears and everything I had encountered in my life, but it seemed he didn't care enough to try to show me something different. I felt lost, stuck, and too afraid to make the wrong choice by walking away.

I feel like I was always on standby, waiting on that thing to go wrong because things were still going strong between us two. It was the longest stretch we had gone without incident, and I didn't want to get too excited and jinx it. However, it felt like breaking down, packing my things up, and walking away had truly made an impact. It took me to stop talking and take action for him to realize that I love him, but I love me more, and enough to walk away if I had to. It took me to break down for us to get to our breakthrough.

Chapter 8

Stop, Settle, Or Step?

I was working and praying to God, seeking my purpose and to better understand the different levels of pain I had endured. I was invited to visit a church by a coworker, and it was during a women's prayer night service. I showed up and the pastor advised they would play a song that night and wanted us to pray that the Holy Spirit visit each one of us and provide the need for whatever we were seeking God for. With an open heart and mind, we were advised to close our eyes and let the song being played speak to us. I remember closing my eyes and not being able to open them. The song being played was "No Weapon" by Fred Hammond. I was immediately overtaken by emotion and started crying silently, but steady tears streamed down my face.

I felt my heart breaking, but the more I cried, the lighter I felt. I saw a whiteboard appear and I heard the Holy Spirit say to me, "This is the last time you will cry about this thing in this way. Let it out and let it go."

Then, all the things I had been through in my life that caused my heart to break and me to feel inadequate and as if I was not and would never be enough filled the board. I saw people who had hurt me. I saw circumstances that were not favorable. I saw my younger self in tears, sad. I saw the number seven, and all the weapons (things they said and did, etc.) that had formed. In one swift movement, He told me He was about to overflow my life with so many blessings, I wouldn't have time to think about the seven years from my childhood I felt was stolen from me or the reasons they didn't protect me or why they were incapable of loving me the way I know I deserved to be loved.

He assured me He blesses his children double for their trouble! He gives us double portions. He told me to just hang tight, better days are coming. No weapon formed back then has prospered, and none in the future will prosper. He assured me that in all the years that I experienced heartbreak, loss, abuse and trauma, I am gaining way more than I ever loss. It doesn't make sense right now, but it will!

He instructed me to no longer say I had lost seven years of my childhood I couldn't get back. Praise me in that Spirit and see what I do next! The tears slowed down, but I cried so much, I felt the lightest I had felt in YEARS! I felt free. Free from all the pain and baggage I had been carrying that was not intended for me to. It was at that very moment in life, I knew, without a doubt, I was coming out of the darkness and entering the light for eternity! No one could tell me different.

As I left that parking lot and drove home, there were so many emotions and thoughts swarming my mind. A simple, "Yes," and being obedient can change your entire path. It is the difference between you staying in the dark and coming toward the light.

I was so thankful for the invite and even more that I was obedient and showed up. I learned how intentional God was on this night! God knew everything I had been through, and He knew what I needed at the right time to carry on and evolve into my next season.

For the first time in my life, I entertained the idea of sitting my mom down and having a sincere, heart to heart about everything that had transpired and my true feelings on how everything was handled from my childhood. I didn't know what words I would say or how she would receive it. All I could think about is not letting one of us leave this Earth before we had this conversation. I thought I had forgiven them both for what they did and did not do regarding this situation. After my experience on that night, I couldn't be so sure. I wanted to make sure I completely freed myself from any of it so I could live freely in the blessings that God had for me and my family.

I knew you couldn't be available to get what God had for you if you didn't forgive others. In my mind, they had already taken up a lot of my time and controlled my choices and everything in between, and I was not going to live like that anymore. As I pulled up to my house, I thanked God for the divine and intentional appointment and for coming to see about me. I needed Him. I needed that experience at that moment and time in my life. So, when people say that God is an on-time God and always has perfect timing, I felt that.

I slept so well that night. No worries, no fears, and in the comfort of my own home.

Within the next few days, I decided it was time, while things were still fresh, to have a talk with my mom. When I went to her house, I asked if she had a moment, and she did. It was the two of us. We had a brief discussion, but my grandmother, who had been diagnosed with dementia, was also there. So, the conversation did not go the way I had hoped, but I was able to let her know I forgave them, and I was thankful and blessed to be the woman I am today, all thanks and credit due to God. I wanted her to understand they got no credit for that.

I explained I felt she let me down regarding how it was handled, but I had to move on. During the conversation, he came upstairs to confirm that everything was OK. We said yes, and shortly after, I got my things and left to head home. In her face, I did not cry, but when I made it home to my husband, I bawled my eyes out. I explained to him that sometimes you just have to be OK with the fact you may never get an apology or acknowledgment for trauma that others inflicted upon you. I advised him I had real hope that my mother and I could be closer than we are and were when I was growing up.

After the conversation, I felt more lost than I did going in because she did what she has always done which is skate around the subject or deflect. I was done with expecting anything more from her and I wiped my eyes, remembering what the Holy Spirit had already confirmed for me regarding the situation. I had to find something to hold on to in order to not go backward.

My husband was able to console me and empathize with the pain I felt. He told me it'll all work out and he admired my strength, despite everything I had been through.

The next morning, my mom called me from her work phone. She must have thought about the conversation we had the night prior. She explained she felt like our relationship was strained because I felt she failed me when it came to that situation. She further stated that she did not understand how this could be the case, but nonetheless, that was where we were. She said it seemed like I felt she failed me as a mother, so she guessed she had.

I explained to her I wouldn't necessarily say she failed me as a mother, but I felt she failed to protect me. We could not go into much more details as she was at work and had other things to address, so we ended the call.

The conversation played on repeat in my head for hours. Eventually, I had to let it go. I didn't want to keep going backward to go nowhere. In my mind, this was a situation where we would always agree to disagree, and the relationship would be what it would be.

I realized I needed to get back to my happy place. I needed God and the guidance of the Holy Spirit to endure this next phase of my life. I went into serious prayer and showed up to church faithfully. My family ended up joining the same church as my parents at the time. While I struggled internally with my mother and I's relationship status, I always fell back into the state of mind of a little girl in her presence.

I was so intentional about my relationship with God, living in the overflow. I had such a peace that was unexplainable. I was so positive, and when negative thoughts would creep in, I learned to master negating it with God's word and recovering my good vibes and energy. Some called me Positive Patty during this season of my life because I rarely ever entertained anything negative. I could spin the worse of the worse into why it was a lesson or blessing for anyone. I spent so much time in my prayer closet at home, the Lord continued to pour into me.

I prayed and said, "Yes and Amen!" to the Lord's will for my life. I meant it with everything in me.

I experienced God on new levels that I never had before. I was being used in so many ways, I knew it had nothing to do with me and I was just the willing vessel. It felt so good to be so connected and in tune with God! I didn't have much time to think about my life, the journey, or the past. I was on a natural high that was so amazing, and I wanted to live there forever.

I was invited to a church by one of my friends. I was obedient and showed up and there was a prophetess there, visiting the church during that service. During the service, there was prayer, then an altar call for anyone who felt the Lord was leading them to go up. This was always a struggle for me, especially earlier in my faith walk. I always assumed people would watch and judge, trying to figure out, *What's wrong with her? What's her story? Why is she going up to the altar?*

For a long time, these thoughts were enough to keep me in my seat. This day, the unction was so strong. I felt the Holy Spirit push me and my feet started going and didn't stop until I reached the front. The prophetess spoke over a couple of people in line before me, and when she saw me, her face lit up and there was a glow like I had never seen before.

She smiled so big and said, "Oh my goodness, you are so special to God. I am not sure what your story is, but you are the apple of His eye. He loves you so much. He wants to use you in such a HUGE way, but He says you struggle with consistency. He wants me to tell you He is waiting on YOU to be more consistent with Him and He will bless you BIG!"

My eyes filled with tears and they streamed down my face. *Lord, You have not forgotten about me and all I have gone through. You love me enough to set up a divine appointment such as this for me. I promise I won't let You down.*

I had a schedule set and started waking up around 3:30 a.m. and would go to my prayer closet until about 5:30 a.m. It felt weird at first. It was quiet. I didn't know what to say. I didn't hear anything from Him, but I continued to show up because it felt right. I took my Bible in on these mornings and my Bible App on my phone. I would sit in there and read the verse of the day and pray and thank God for keeping me and my family safe. I would thank Him for the woman I was, despite the storms and struggles. Some days, tears would stream down my face and that was the two-hour experience. Other times, I would pray for whatever was on my heart. I would ask for God to use me like He wanted to.

One day, when I woke up, something different happened. I immediately started hearing insightful words that would come so fast, I had to grab my phone and start typing them. I could not go back to sleep if I tried. Sometimes, I would be so exhausted and try to think I would remember it when I woke up, but it was so persistent, I could not sleep until I got it out.

God was pleased with me. He was pleased with my intentional effort and consistency to show up, no matter what. I heard the Holy Spirit confirm that so clearly for me.

He said, "Now, I can use you."

God gave me these messages that would come to me in the wee hours of the morning every day in 2018. Initially, I did not know what I was supposed to do with them, but I prayed for clarity and direction.

I remember asking God, "What if I run out of things to say?"

He replied, "You have Me, so you will never have to worry about this. This is not a 'you' thing. Just keep Me first and don't get caught up in anything else. Trust that it will reach whoever it needs to reach. If only one is reached, then the job is done. It's always going to be an on-time word and people will still be blessed by them in the years to come when I have elevated you to other things. Trust me."

I then started posting them every day on Facebook. I remember asking God for guidance and allowing Him to lead me every step of the way. That year was such a blessing to me. The best part for me was that every morning, I would receive a download from the Lord, and I was able to allow each word to minister to me first, before I even thought to share with others. Only after I received what I was supposed to would I feel comfortable sharing with others.

This was very important because I had encountered so many people in the church who were comfortable giving advice, sharing what the Lord told them about another person, and pointing fingers at everything else that is "wrong", but struggled with understanding their flaws. This process taught me how to really take a hard look at myself and allow God to change the one part I could control, which was me.

That entire year, God dealt with me about me. He showed me myself in ways I could never have seen through anyone else's lens. God confirmed for me who I am to Him and allowed me to see myself the way He sees me. He saw me well beyond the shame, brokenness, and flaws. He saw a willing vessel who was able to find beauty in the brokenness from the master Himself.

I had so many conversations with God in this season of my

life. I was overwhelmed in an amazing way! I remember talking with God one day and hearing a key drop. I closed my eyes and saw a key ring full of keys and heard so clearly, "I have all these things for you, and it's yours. All you have to do is not go against what you know is right. It doesn't matter what everyone else around you is doing. You must commit to not compromising, no matter what."

My response that changed everything was, "Yes and Amen."

God taught me, in life, I have three options: stop, settle, or step. He loved on me and showed me that the pain I felt was due to me not being able to fully forgive those who had hurt me and let me down. But, more importantly, I had not forgiven myself. He assured me that the reason I could not do this was because I didn't know how to. At least until now, there had not been a good blueprint provided to me. I cried and told God I felt like I had forgiven them. He assured me that in due time, I would be able to do this.

In this season of my life, He wanted me to focus on my relationship with Him and being consistent in that. So, I did. He wanted me to confirm if I was going to stop, settle, or step?

June 2018 - I received a message from a young lady who owned an International Radio Network, who was Spirit-led to reach out to me to extend an opportunity to join her network. I was so nervous but found comfort in the fact I knew to pray and seek God. He approved and He had already given me the name of the segment, "Let's Talk", a short while before she had reached out.

There had always been this shadow of fear hanging over me, scared to speak up, stand up, and share my full testimony because it would make my parents mad, uncomfortable, and risked people finding out the deep, dark family secret. I shared parts of my testimony along the way to help certain people, but always holding back the full facts in fear of the backlash or my parents getting in trouble or ruining their image and reputation they had created.

As a part of a Christian music group, I couldn't fully share my testimony in song due to always considering if my parents would consider it "too close to home". I tried to protect them and the image they had painted for everyone else who was not "in the loop" of what really happened.

The expectation my whole life was that we swept it under the rug and were to act like a normal, well put together family, despite this big elephant in every room.

I enjoyed the opportunity to be used by God. The blessings kept flowing and I was content being obedient and sharing whatever word God saw fit. The only problem was, I avoided talking about my truth. I enjoyed encouraging and celebrating other people breaking free from their strongholds and still held shame about my past at the same time.

I found a sister in Christ who changed my life and she believed in and poured into me faithfully. We laughed, prayed, and cried together on multiple occasions. It felt so good to experience a genuine person who loved God as much as I did.

I had made a choice that stopping or settling wasn't an option and that no matter what, I would keep stepping.

Chapter 9

Faith Fuel Stop

The pain that still exists from losing our first born... (September 3, 2021)

Anxiety is REAL. I've been advised that, to some degree, it's necessary to have it. It's what helps us to be vigilant and aware that something is off within us. However, too much of anything is not good. We must be careful not to allow it to overtake or overwhelm us. When this happens, it actually robs us of the opportunity we have to live in the moment.

I am learning that I can live in this moment of what's actually happening without discarding what happened before. It doesn't make it any less my truth, BUT GOD has allowed me to see and experience His love, grace, and mercy, which gives me HOPE and the will to hold on to my FAITH through this process. I am ALLOWED and have the AUTHORITY to expect GOD to come through and deliver again. I am allowed to acknowledge the reality of what happened while still being happy and enjoying this experience that God has blessed us with.

I choose the path of healing and we are responsible for our

own and the process that comes with that. I choose to relax and take a deep breath (sometimes multiple) to lessen the stress by remembering who GOD is and has been to me and my family! He is smiling down and blessing us abundantly and exceedingly above what we could ever ask for. I'm able to accept this and own the part I'm to play to get to the promise.

God is faithful even when we are not. God loves us. He is blessing abundantly and delivering us from anxiety in this season. If we only believe and trust that HE can, then He will.

Anxiety is REAL, but our GOD is BIGGER, and we can walk in our VICTORY NOW!!!

Dear Queen, (January 17, 2022)

You've traveled a rough road, but you never gave up. Although we couldn't always see God's "better", we made it through all kinds of crazy weather. What I'm most thankful for in this moment is my choices to be intentional to keep betting on me, no matter the circumstances. The enemy has been at me for a very long time, but my GOD keeps showing up for me OVER AND OVER AGAIN! The best thing I did for myself was focus on healing for real and owning my truth for what it is. I'm the best person to walk in these shoes because I understand there is purpose in the pain. I know nothing and no one is perfect. I love hard and beyond limits. I forgive the unforgivable. I choose to let God fight my battles because HE handles them! I missed this glow! I missed my shine. Yeah, I took a season off to get refocused but now I'm back and I'm better than last time!

My message to you in this season is to be intentional and heal for real. Know and own your truth so you can grow. *Really* grow.

"Worry Not & Worship" (October 10, 2018)

So often, we worry about things that don't even matter.

Concern yourself with the things Christ wants you to be considerate of. The way we treat others, the way we love, the way we live, the way we give, and everything in between.

Don't Stop. Don't Settle. Keep Stepping.

Today Is "Scars Should..." Saturday (October 27, 2018)

Some scars are physical, mental, and/or emotional. The things we go through can either make us better or bitter.

In life, some scars serve as a traumatic reminder, while others are less traumatic. We each take in and categorize these scars differently.

People can help push us to a point where we question if we do or don't have a purpose to fulfill. Don't give people that kind of power over you when it pertains to your purpose! God is the only one that has the power to determine this, and HE already decided and NO HE hasn't changed His mind! Go and be great simply because God said you can be!

Abuse, rejection, love loss, guilt, shame and low self-esteem are some results and things that trigger these scars.

No matter what you've experienced up to this point, understand your God is bigger than any and all of it.

When we reflect over our lives, what scars are hindering you from walking and moving forward into what God has called you to do?

"Don't allow them (scars) to defeat, destroy, and determine your destiny."

- Shae Pratcher -

"Scars should serve as a reminder that we've experienced some storms, BUT GOD still saved and kept us in and through them."

- Shae Pratcher -

Don't Stop. Don't Settle. Keep Stepping.

Aug 14, 2021

Healing is necessary to stop the hurt. It's a choice we have, and the process is not pretty. However, to be the best version of YOU that God created, letting go and letting Him lead you from that place is the best choice YOU can make.

There comes a time when you have to stop putting the ball in everyone else's court, expecting something from them that may never happen. It's then you can truly focus on the things that matter and that will help you be a better individual overall. For me, it's being a better woman of God, a better wife, and mother.

Hurt people, hurt people, BUT HEALED people, help people.

God is good! He is able. He is faithful! Hold on a little longer because the storm is passing over in Jesus's mighty, matchless name, AMEN.

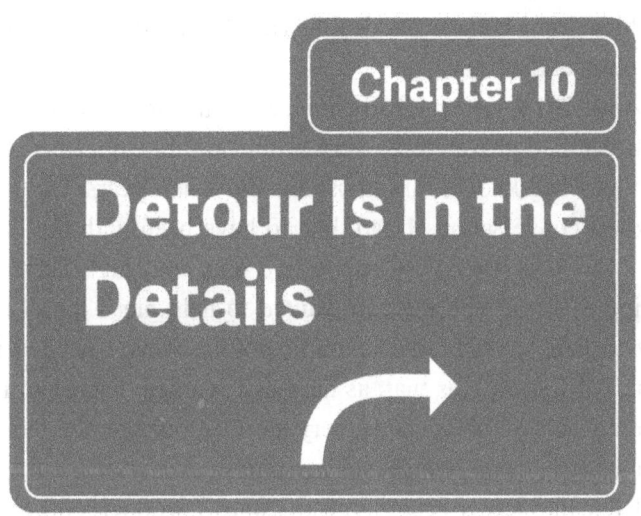

Chapter 10
Detour Is In the Details

It was around February and March 2019 when I realized how much I had going on. I was a full-time employee, host of the "Let's Talk" radio show, Mary Kay consultant, full-time mother and wife, college student, and entrepreneur. I was exhausted and knew I was coming to a crossroads when it impacted my husband and kids the most. I had a hard choice to make because I had taken on too much at one time. I had to go into serious prayer because I needed help to determine what I needed to let go. I didn't want to let anything go or anyone down because so many people depended on me.

I remember breaking down crying in my prayer closet occasionally because someone was going to be impacted by the decision I needed to make. I tried to think through it logically, and I prayed to God for clarity. I remember driving to work and hearing so clearly, "Your assignment here is over." I looked around that parking lot and just knew I had hallucinated because this was my whole job that paid ALL my bills.

I turned my car off and proceeded like it was just another day. The more days that went by, I realized I needed to make a choice that would help allow me more flexibility with my family.

Working from home was ideally what I needed, which was not an option at that time.

April 2019, the time had come, and I had to walk away from a job that had proven to be very promising for my career. It had been all I had known for almost six and a half years. One of the toughest conversations I had, had to have been with the leadership who had been very supportive and amazing! They were willing to work with me and wanted to help me. I didn't know how to help myself, so I couldn't outline what I needed from them. All I knew was that, as hard as I worked, I felt like I was winning at everything and everyone else, except for the ones who mattered most, which was my family.

I felt like I was losing with the ones I worked hard for and had to weigh if it was worth it or not. My honest answer to myself was no. I did not want to be the mom who was there physically but never there emotionally to nurture and care for them the way they needed. I wasn't OK with sacrificing their needs for my wants because I had made a promise to be better for them. My parents were both in the military and missed much of our lives, and I believed that played a role in our strained relationships as well.

Tears welled up in my eyes and streamed down my face as I prepped myself to share the news with my team, and we all cried. This was what I was passionate about: my people. They worked hard with and for me. I believed if you took care of your people, they would work hard for you and that proved to be the case for the team of people I worked with. I thought about the trenches we had been in and overcome together. I thought about the countless times I said, "Teamwork makes the dream work!" The attitude was, we win together, we lose together. I was never someone who was above doing what I asked them to do. From a career stance, this was a painful part of my process that I had to endure.

This was another hard moment in my life and the only thing

that made it easier was because I knew I was being obedient and believed that somehow, it would work out.

I started working a full-time remote job, which allowed me to be more in the moment with my family and balance the multiple roles I had taken on. In time, things got better at home, and I wasn't as stressed or stretched thin. My kids were so happy we could spend more time together and that I was more available and able to be more in the moment. We embraced this time spent, and although I missed my career, the people, and environment at Agero, I coped with the new norm.

About six months later (October 2019), another opportunity to serve became available for another radio show ministry for a large gospel station, V1075, based out of Atlanta, GA. I prayed about this one, and again, what a blessing and awesome experience it was. The name of my radio show segment was "Praying Partners", and I was able to interview celebrities such as Terri J. Vaughn and Erica Campbell, prayed for so many, laughed, and experienced a real sense of being connected and committed to God on a new level.

Here I was, finally moving forward in a positive direction and being used by God in a huge way. I was encouraged so much by the motivational FB posts, both radio shows, "Let's Talk" and "Praying Partners", as well as praying with and for my family and friends daily.

I felt as though I'd grasped hold to any and everything that gave me hope toward a fruitful future.

Then, Covid hit in 2019-2020 and life changed for my family drastically. Kids switched to virtual school abruptly, which worked because I was already working from home, but I was laid off from my job due to Covid in 2020.

I started back working at Agero in June 2020, which was my preferred career choice. I had grown on so many levels with this company, so to go back was surreal and exciting for me!

I returned, but not in the leadership capacity I once held as I wanted to ease my way back in, and through prayer, God said not now. I came back to the care team, humbly working through the high priority cases for nine months before I was promoted to client services, which had been a goal of mine. It felt like where I belonged and like a void had been filled when I joined the team that welcomed me with open arms!

"It was at this time, satisfaction was starting to show itself in my life again. Things were definitely turning around. One thing I have learned is that seasons change. We must learn to take the good with the bad and vice versa because the detour is in the details. Depending on our attitude and posture, it'll dictate if there will be a delay or denial along the way toward our destiny."

~ Shae Pratcher ~

Chapter 11

Just Us

January 2021, I woke up to log into work one day and I was so scatterbrained. I couldn't put anything together and nothing made sense at a job I had been at for eight plus years. I felt nauseous and like I wanted to pass out at the same time. It was a familiar feeling, but I remember saying out loud, "Is that even possible?"

I pulled out my calendar and looked at the date, trying to mentally track when I had last seen "Ms. Flow" and realized I was late. I was typically in sync with a couple of friends and family members, so I remembered texting to confirm if they had already had theirs for the month or if I was tripping. Anxiously, I sat, staring at my phone, watching and waiting for a reply for confirmation. My heart dropped when I received confirmation from one that it had already come and gone for the month. My eyes were so BIG, and I immediately found myself on the bathroom floor, tossing things around, looking for the last pregnancy test I had for a time such as this. I finally found it and went to put it to the test.

As I peed on the stick, I remember thinking I needed to make a doctor's appointment to get back on birth control. Just as I was trying to get the cap back on to set it on the side until the results were ready, two lines popped up! I had to rub my eyes and pinch myself to confirm I was not dreaming. It was true, I was pregnant again.

I was in no place mentally to even fully comprehend what this meant and how we were going to adjust. Our older kids were in virtual school since the pandemic had started and I was finally able to work from home, but the job had been emailing about the process for migrating back to the building in waves.

I stood up and rushed to wake my husband up to tell him the news. I showed him the test and he said, "OK," and rolled over to go back to sleep as he worked an alternate shift than I did.

I stood over him in shock. Sleep was not on the radar for me, so I shook him.

I said, "OK? What? Like, what are we going to do?"

He said, "What do you mean? There's only one thing we can do." He assured me he had no worries, and we would be just fine.

I made a doctor's appointment. They confirmed I was pregnant and referred me to the OBGYN and the special clinic as I was high risk since our first born had Trisomy thirteen. Additionally, I already had three C-sections, and this would make it the fourth. I had so many emotions running through me, and my mind was all over the place. I was happy about the baby but worried about the process and stages of the pregnancy as it was always stressful for us as a family.

I thought about many things in that moment. It had been my experience that when I got pregnant, my husband and I had all kinds of tests and trials. It felt like that was when the enemy found his way in through the cracks and crevices.

I felt myself getting worked up, concerned about what curve balls the enemy would throw our way this time.

Next, I heard the Holy Spirit say, "No fire can burn you and no battle can turn you!"

I whispered to myself, "You got this because God's got you," as tears streamed down my face and my heart beat fast.

Then, God reminded me of just how faithful He had been to my family. He allowed me to sit and reflect on how much we had endured TOGETHER. He reminded me I needed to take a deep breath and remember He is God all by Himself and all I needed to do was my part and leave the rest to Him. Although this pregnancy wasn't planned, it was definitely purposeful. I smiled. I love how gentle God is with me.

I had a pep talk with myself to accept God's will and go with the flow. I promised myself I would not stress about things that had not manifested. I needed to trust God the same way I had throughout my life.

I told myself my husband and I had matured and were not in the same place and space we had been in years ago. No matter what the enemy threw our way, there was nothing we couldn't overcome or get through because we had made a vow to face the world together.

Even in the hardest moments, we chose to stand together and put a praise on it! The things that had broken other marriages apart helped us to see at the end of the day, it was always JUST US! No matter who had come in our lives and walked out for whatever reason, we still had each other. We had taken many losses, but the one thing that kept us winning was that it was always us for us. We love us! We choose us! It was our daily prayer that when all else failed, it would always be JUST US, forever plus a day, times infinity.

It wasn't long until we were both head over heels about our growing family. We were in bed one night and he looked me in my face and said, "I know the baby's name. At least the first name, anyway."

I remember thinking, *Oh, Lord, please let us agree about this.*

I looked over at him and said, "What is it?"

He said, "Justus, spelled like JUST US."

I stared at him for a minute, then he said, "Through everything we have been through, we overcame and continue to do so, and it's always been Just Us."

I instantly fell in LOVE with it and that was what we agreed to name our last born, Justus.

"SOMETIMES IN LIFE CHAOS STRIKES, AND THINGS SEEM hectic. My greatest testimonies have come from the things that hurt me the most and the deepest. Having children has been a struggle for me, and accepting my past has been painful, but both have pushed me into my purpose.

In and through it all, the one thing that's been consistent and faithful is God. What has carried me through up to now is the fact that it's always been Just Us. When everyone and everything else fails, God doesn't."

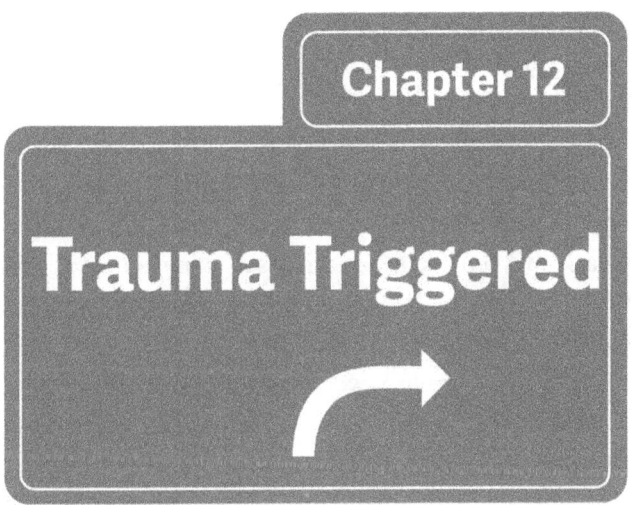

Chapter 12
Trauma Triggered

On many days, I had to stifle thoughts to try to allow my kids to have a relationship with my parents, despite being uncomfortable due to the pain I felt as a child. I prayed hard that deep down, my kids never crossed that bridge and never had any traumatic experiences that cost them their peace of mind and joy. These experiences had a way of robbing you of not only your childhood and innocence, but also the way you see the world going forward.

There were so many things that went through my mind once I started having kids. Do I keep them from them? Do I give them a chance to get to know them? How do I protect them from the ugly truth? What's the right thing to do?

Even in all that I went through, I tried for years to allow them both to be grandparents. I considered the damage, impact, and affect it would have on my kids if I didn't at least try. I gave it all I had, despite all the extra effort I had to put in to make it happen.

I drove across town with my kids to ensure they spent time together. I answered their calls. While they were in their presence, I tried to be in multiple places at once to ensure my kids never had the same experiences I did. I had to make sure they were safe. There was always that thought in my mind, and I got tired of living like that.

When my daughter turned seven, it hit me hard because that was around the age the molestation started for me. My mom started reaching out, asking to keep my kids overnight. She would ask to keep them and then say things such as, "Well, I have to go get my nails done in the morning, but your dad will be here with them until I get back."

In my mind, I could never understand how she could think that would be OK or an option for me, understanding what happened to me. I would find ways to say no creatively at first to try to keep the peace and not address the elephant in the room because she never liked discussing it.

One day in early 2021, it hit me hard when she asked me again to keep my kids overnight. I was sitting at home and had to be honest with myself. Was I willing to sacrifice my kids for her feelings? What kind of mother was I to leave my kids overnight, knowing what could happen, especially with my daughter being around the same age I was when it started happening to me? I made a commitment to protect my kids, by any means necessary, and if that meant standing up to my parents, then so be it. It was my responsibility to protect my kids and speak up for them, and if I didn't, shame on me.

It was at that point I knew I had to sit down and have a hard talk with my mom and be candid. I talked with my husband, and he assured me he supported whatever I wanted to do. He understood and agreed that we couldn't put our kids in harm's way like that.

Honestly, I had buckled under pressure too many times in my life. When it only impacted me, that was one thing, but when it came to my kids, I'd pull strength from somewhere every single time.

So, I went over to my mom's house and asked her if we

could chat alone for a minute. She said her usual, "Uh oh, it must be bad. Is it going to upset me?"

I replied, "It honestly might, but it's one of those things we have to talk about."

I started out letting her know I loved her very much and wanted her to know that the conversation had been overdue, but needed to happen. She cut me off, saying I didn't have to say all that and to just get to what I needed to say. I told her it concerned her recent requests to keep my kids overnight.

"I'm not comfortable doing this, due to what happened to me as a little girl. It's my job to protect my kids and I must do what I feel is right." I further explained that it had taken me some time to sift through what was the right thing and I felt I'd been more than fair by allowing them to have a relationship with my kids. I advised for the relationship with my kids to continue, she and I must be on the same page. I explained I didn't feel like we were and gave some examples of why I felt that way. One of those was how she asked to keep my kids overnight but said things like she had errands to run or was going to get her nails done and that my dad would be there with them until she got back. There was no reassurance of their safety, and I didn't know if it was because it had been swept under the rug that she felt it wouldn't happen, but it happened to me, his biological daughter. Due to this, I couldn't be naive in thinking it couldn't or wouldn't happen to my kids by him.

She advised that even if she said she was going to get her nails done, my daughter would go with her, and I should have known that. I didn't make any assumptions, but the fact that she was okay with leaving my son alone with him still triggered me. Instead of addressing my concerns, she said she figured I had an issue with them keeping my kids, which was why she never asked. By the end of the conversation, she made it clear that if I felt my kids weren't safe, I should keep them home and I couldn't have agreed more. My mom didn't feel she should be stressed while watching her grandchildren. She didn't think she needed to be overly concerned about leaving her grandchildren alone with my father if they so happened to be in the same space together.

My response was, "But you should because you made the choice to stay with him after what he did. It's your job to ensure nothing happens to my kids if they are in your care, but you're right, you shouldn't be stressed out watching my kids. So, there will not be any overnight stays or unattended stays. When I come, they come. When I go, they go."

She replied, "I understand and respect your decision. Those are your kids, and you must do what you have to do. No issue."

She mentioned something about him noticing the difference in us not coming around as much and she had made up some excuse. It wasn't for me to respond or internalize. She said I was having this conversation with her and not him, which made it hard when we knew he loved his grandkids. I explained to her I was having the conversation with her because she was the one who asked to keep them, not him. He'd never do that.

We went our separate ways, and I got my kids and drove back to our house. The drive home seemed long as I replayed the conversation in my head. I couldn't help but think about some things she said, considering what she knew had happened to me. I remember thinking, *She doesn't get it. After all this time, she still just doesn't get it.*

It was at that moment, I felt like I couldn't worry about it and needed to protect my kids unapologetically.

In that moment, things changed. We barely went around as much as we had in the past. There was a sense of peace I felt while being in the comfort of my own home that I grew to love. I was safe. My kids were safe. Life was good. Different, but good.

Chapter 13

The Sit Down

The second half of 2021 was very interesting and stressful for me. I was carrying our pleasant surprise, Baby Justus. Even though I didn't overwhelm myself with many thoughts from my past, there were some natural things I concerned myself with. I had the usual thoughts and anxieties that had become my norm during pregnancy because of the experiences I'd had with past pregnancies. I trusted God, and at the same time, I wanted to keep myself in check in case something tragic happened. I didn't want to feel that same level of pain ever again. I counted my blessings and reminded myself often how blessed I was to carry another baby and was around seven months into the journey at this point. I felt very optimistic.

It felt like a wave of disaster was headed my way and I could not shake the feeling. I kept telling myself to try not to stress or worry about it because the same God who had kept me to this point was still in control. I calmed down and things mellowed out a little.

Then, a family gathering happened. I was so happy to see family members I had not seen in some time. Covid really had a way of putting extra distance in relationships. It wasn't all bad, either. Sometimes you realize seasons change.

In the midst of the family getting together, a topic of the past occurred. In this deep conversation, I learned that what happened to me as a little girl had a lasting negative impact on many others. There were discussions about what we had done in hopes of overcoming and the topic of forgiveness was even mentioned. I felt as though I had forgiven my parents for what happened to me. I did believe I had gotten to a great place in my life, considering all things that had occurred.

The thing was, during this, I realized the pain extended well past me and my life. I learned of some struggles that other family members had with knowing that this had happened. The topic was one that did not come up often at all. We realized, though that we were "allowed" to have those conversations and to express how we felt, although that had not been an option in the past. This was hard. It hurt. They cried and it upset me, and I cried. It was in that moment, I felt something different.

I realized that part of my life was still a very sore and raw subject for me. I was able to clearly identify that my soul needed to have this moment to realize of where I needed God to do a work in me. I remember thinking, *I wish I could take all this pain away from everyone.*

Truth was, when I thought it only impacted me, I could somehow deal with it and move on with my life to the best of my ability. That mindset allowed me to suppress those thoughts and feelings. I buried them in a place that almost made them nonexistent. It was the best thing I could do as a child and it was honestly how I made it through.

As I grew older, it only came to the surface and showed its face when I was triggered by a feeling, a thought, or an experience that forced me to remember bits and pieces. It was on this day, I realized a deeper conversation needed to happen for those family members who still felt bothered with the way everything unfolded.

I had already had the difficult conversations I needed to have with my parents and had forgiven them. They knew where I stood with the situation, and I was now focusing on the way ahead and being intentional about breaking generational curses. It stopped with me. My kids wouldn't have this same experience.

I made it clear I supported and respected whatever choice they made to try to obtain a level of peace to move forward. I stressed the fact that it had been a rocky road for me, and it wasn't easy, but I was finally at a place in my life where I had to make a choice to understand I couldn't change the past and had to focus on what I could do to heal and press into my purpose. They acknowledged and commended me on the growth and shared how proud they were of the woman I had become, despite everything. God got all the credit and the glory because, in my own strength, I could've never done it.

We talked into the wee hours of the next morning, having this long, overdue conversation that ultimately sparked a new light within me. After realizing what time it was, I wobbled my pregnant self to bed. Honestly, I went to bed feeling a little scrambled about what would come next. I believed everything happened for a reason and trusted nothing happened by mistake. I knew the Holy Spirit would provide clarity into what I was supposed to do with this situation that had occurred.

Over the next few weeks, I realized that more of these conversations were happening. Additional family members were made aware and hearts weighed heavily on people. I remember feeling like things were going to explode. I was instantly stressed, but felt everyone had the right to handle things the way they felt was necessary to cope with it. I made a choice at that point to let go and let God. I decided I had to stop being in defense mode and I was intentional about not being like my parents. My prayer was and still is, "Yes and Amen."

I agreed to do whatever God wanted me to do to fulfill the purpose that was connected to His will for my life. With that came the understanding that I must be willing to do what He wanted me to do, which may not be comfortable to me.

Considering those conversations, I felt that another sit down with my mother needed to happen. I agreed to go with the other person due to how things had unraveled in the past. We did not want to deal with the "he said", "she said", and "they said" drama that could come with the situation to possibly deflect.

Pregnant and stressed was an understatement for the way I felt at this stage in my life. However, I looked at the bigger picture and knew this conversation had the potential to push us into the next stage of the process, whatever that looked like. Sometimes, we feel like we need closure and that can only be done by standing up to face the fear head on or sitting down and being direct about your stance. It was not easy when dealing with people who didn't see things the way you do. It was not easy when you were talking about the hard things that had been off limits all your life. It was not easy when it was with the person who brought you into this world and you know it would be hard for them to hear it. Nonetheless, you realize that getting to a place of healing, it was something you must do.

We made the trip over to her house together hoping she would be there. We called her phone once we had arrived, and she opened the door for us. Her response was that it must be something because we had come together. The other party explained that this would be a rough conversation, but it was one we felt was necessary.

We all sat down and the other party started the conversation off by setting the tone for how we would like the conversation to go. They realized there would be some new information shared, along with some information she was aware of from the past and then the outcome of what all this meant. They advised this was not an easy conversation to have, but out of respect for her, we felt it needed to happen. They went into details about this being regarding the experience that came to light with my father.

They shared detailed information about things that had transpired that should not have, unrelated to me. They explained where they felt the relationship status stood and the reason why. Then the conversation shifted to what happened to me as a little girl and how many of our family members seemed to know a lot of details about what transpired that they were not aware of. This was a big reason for the conversation, as the information raised deep concerns.

In considering the level of what happened, there was no way, in good faith, children could be in that kind of environment any longer. There were some changes we felt needed to be made to protect the younger children in the family. My mom interjected in a mellow tone and said she understood and respected whatever decision needed to be made, just as she had previously told me. She advised she didn't like that it had to be this way, but she respected it. She mentioned she felt like she was being held responsible and punished for things she did not do. She wanted to understand what exactly we were holding her accountable for in this whole situation.

I felt she failed to protect me once she knew what happened. She allowed my dad to come back into the household. Her rebuttal was that she wished we had said something back in the day if we were not OK with the decision. After all, she reminded us the decision to allow him to come back was a choice each of us made as a family. The other party explained that, as kids, that wasn't a decision that should have been ours to make. Up to that point, we had never been a part of any decisions.

I had, indeed, spoken up after the choice was made, shortly after he had returned. I pulled her to the side and explained I was not doing too well with him being back, which she responded to by threatening to turn herself in to her commander and authorities, and calling my grandfather. There was an in-depth conversation between my grandfather and myself, which ended with me realizing my only option was to suck it up.

As a child, I did not want her to go to jail for this, so I had to deal with it, but none of us got any help. No therapy. No professional help. The other party expressed the impacts that this situation had on their lives personally and it brought tears to my eyes. No one should have had to endure that kind of thing, and yet here we were, about twenty years later, having this conversation.

My mother expressed that she wished she had turned herself in so she wouldn't be dealing with this now. To her, the subject kept coming up and she couldn't understand why, but it was because the subject was never fully addressed. I believed she wanted to continue to keep it buried under the rug, but she had people from church bringing their kids around without knowing what happened, and it wasn't right. My concern grew when I realized a certain church member had grown very attached and they had kids. I didn't want that on my conscience, but she assured me what went on in her household was of no concern for me.

She shared how much they loved their grandkids and how she had been making up excuses to my father about why we hadn't been coming around lately. We hadn't been coming around lately because I didn't feel comfortable. She wanted me to believe if it happened again, the outcome would be different from before, but that was the problem. I didn't want there to be a "next time."

We chose to look at the situation from the lens of being parents. We couldn't have our kids in that environment, risking what may happen. Again, she stated she respected our decision and an awkward silence followed before she began crying and apologizing. She explained this was the consequence of the choice she made, but she felt she was being punished. The other party attempted to explain that the intent was not to "punish" her, but to make the right choice for their grandkids.

My mother said that everyone continued to have the talk with her, but nobody addressed with him and she wouldn't be the one to do so, knowing it would lead to him becoming agitated and frustrated.

The other party was frank in stating they had no intention of bringing the subject up to him, and they'd only addressed it with her because of the love and respect they had for her, which didn't exist for my father. I was eager to have a conversation with my father as there were some things I felt he needed to know. I assured her I would set the same expectations with him so that it was clear where I stood with my decision as it pertained to protecting my children.

Shortly after this, we decided it was time to part ways. Hugs were exchanged and we got in our cars and drove away.

I was alone with my thoughts in my car, admitting that while others could empathize and show sympathy, it was my truth. I had to take ownership in what my future looked like. I couldn't expect anyone else to feel or understand the depths of the pain I had endured. The level of disappointment I had experienced was not something I could put into words to make sense to anyone else.

I finally realized I had been walking around with not only a broken heart, but it was also scarred and beaten up. I recognized the level of hurt was being shielded by the survival coping mechanisms I had mastered. Just because I had learned how to mask it didn't mean it didn't matter and that it didn't exist. I had learned how to put on a face that said I was OK on the outside, even though inside, I was dying.

I didn't want sympathy. I didn't want people to judge me. I didn't want to make waves, but I needed to heal, for real. As I thought back over my life, it was ironic how many times God had used me to speak to someone else's pain, disappointment, let down, among all the other emotions.

However, the real question was, "God, can we sit down so I can understand what You want to say to me about me?" I wanted to know. I *needed* to know...

Chapter 14
The Stand Up

Over the next few days after the sit down with my mom, my heart was heavy. It always amazed me how the aftereffects lingered long after the conversation was over. It baffled me that after all I'd gone through, she didn't feel it was her responsibility to have a conversation with my father about the reason we were deciding to pull back and not come around. I replayed it over and over because I knew it was another hard conversation I was bound to have to have with him myself.

If it were up to me, I was ready to have it via FaceTime. I was done being uncomfortable. I just wanted to be honest and get off my chest what I'd needed to say for many years, but never had the courage or strength to in the past.

After a few days of going back and forth with myself, I decided and there was no better time than now to make the call.

He answered the FaceTime call and I asked if he was free to talk, making an observation that he was at work, but in his truck by himself. I explained I had some things I needed to talk to him about after speaking with my mom about what happened to me during my childhood and there were some things that had not been said that I needed to let him know. He stopped me and said he understood, but preferred to talk about it in person. He also immediately told me he was in a different space in his life and humble enough to be open to what I had to say. Apparently, he'd had a breakthrough in church and advised that he realized there were some things he could have and wanted to share with his children now.

My expression was stoic as he talked about how he had been molested, but finally decided to speak up when he was fifteen. This wasn't news to me because my mother had already shared this with me back when I was younger. I recalled the compassion she had in her voice when she told me. The thing was, all I could muster up to say was that, while he may have felt that helped put things in perspective for me, it hadn't. In fact, it did the opposite. I couldn't respect or appreciate people deflecting, and the fact he knew how it felt to go through such trauma and he could inflict the same pain on me made it worse, in my opinion.

Before abruptly ending the call, he assured me he wanted to talk but it would have to be in person and he'd contact me soon so we could arrange a day and time to do so.

On July 26, 2021, my dad reached out and agreed to meet at my house. I remember feeling faint and a feeling rush over me before he arrived. I let my husband know he was coming over so we could talk, but it was going to be outside. I went outside and was immediately taken aback by the heat that hit me. I was about seven months pregnant with our fourth baby. I felt nauseous at the thought that I was having to have yet another stressful conversation about my past, but it was necessary.

I walked out of my garage door and he pulled me up a chair and stood next to me. I explained to him why I felt the discussion was a must at this point, and I advised him I was going to be very honest. I told him that in the past, he had apologized, and that was fine, but there was some real pain and long-term effects I still experienced due to what he had done to me as a child. He seemed nervous and kept looking around like he thought someone was listening. I had my phone with me, and he asked me if it was on. I flashed it to show him I wasn't recording him or whatever he thought. He then asked me if I minded getting up and walking to the end of the driveway to continue the conversation. It irritated me because I was big and pregnant, and I felt like, once again, it was about control. Nonetheless, I got up from the chair and walked to the end of my driveway to continue the conversation with him.

He said he would let me talk and get out what I had to say and try not to interrupt me. However, he said when I was done, he had something to share with me. I explained to him the conversation was coming up because having my own kids and my daughter being around the age of when the molestation happened to me really weighed heavy on me. I started thinking about my role and responsibility as a mother and it was my number one job to protect them, by any means necessary. I advised him I couldn't, in good faith, think that there was no possibility he wouldn't do the same thing to any of my kids. I advised him the reality was that neither one of us had gotten help and that was something that had always bothered me. How could something be that deeply rooted, and we sweep it under the rug and never seek help? How can anyone be sure it wouldn't happen again?

I told him I was his biological daughter and it happened to me, so I couldn't turn my cheek and think it couldn't or wouldn't happen to my kids. I informed him that those reasons led to additional conversations with my mom recently to let her know I couldn't leave my kids unattended or overnight with them.

Once I was done, he acknowledged the things I said and agreed. Like my mom, he claimed to respect the choice I made and assured me he loved his grandkids. However, he also realized he messed up with his children and had been trying to make amends through his grandchildren. While I understood his point of view, it wasn't something I was willing to risk, and I told him as much.

In life, people do things to others and never understand the true impact it had on their lives. I let him know my spouse knew and had known for a very long time about everything. I explained that this was pertinent information that I knew I had to share with him prior to us getting married.

For so long, he had been forced to function in dysfunction because of the love he had for me. In hindsight, that was not fair to him or our family, and moving forward, we wouldn't do it any longer. We would no longer learn how to be comfortable in dysfunction because that was what it had been.

I explained that intimate things I should be able to enjoy with my husband had been snatched, due to what he had done to me. I explained the relationship with my kids were different because I was so worried about being appropriate and determined to break these generational curses. I told him I'd had to have the "good touch and bad touch" conversations with my kids at an early age to try to protect them, and rebutted my statement by saying, with this day and age, I would have had these kinds of conversations with them early, anyway.

Keeping his grandchildren from him was a good thing, he said. He said it would help him on his journey and allow God to deal with him, so he wanted us to continue to stand on that decision.

Although he positioned himself as someone who understood and respected my decision, he made comments that made me believe otherwise. He mentioned, we thought we were "hard", but we were cut from the same cloth as him as we were a part of him. I ignored the comment. He said he felt this was all coming back up because I wanted to make sure people believed me. I interjected and assured him that part of my life was way over. I wasn't a little girl anymore and I knew, he knew, and God knew what really happened, so that was not what was going on.

It had been brushed under the rug for so long and we hadn't dealt with it. That was why it was coming back up, I had informed him. I had learned to cope with the pain over the years, and when I felt it only impacted me, I was willing to "deal" with it. However, I learned that because of the decisions made back then, other family members were also impacted. I didn't go into details about their struggles because that wasn't my place to share it with him. However, I must take a stand for myself to let them know things didn't just go away for me, and it truly had caused me a lot of grief and heartache in more than one aspect of my life.

He cut me off and said that one of my siblings had other issues going on, so it was easy to deflect and blame it on the past. Bringing my mom into the conversation, he didn't let me forget that she also played a role and how difficult our relationship was. He was quick to remind me that it was he who had come to my rescue when she called me out of my name.

There was no denying that my mother also played a role in my childhood trauma, but as adults, they should have made better choices when handling what happened to me. In my opinion, they both failed to protect me.

It seemed, instead of seeing I was the who had been wronged, he somehow wanted to be the victim. He brought up the fact he felt something was up because all of us kids stopped responding to his daily morning text messages around the same time. I assured him I was my own person and had had no conversations with my siblings about not responding to his daily morning messages, I just decided I needed to focus on my healing, and part of the process was to disconnect from some things. My choice was personal.

Even a dog in the street gets acknowledged, was his comeback. He felt slighted, but I used the opportunity to advise him I couldn't appreciate the messages, to be honest, and would prefer he stop sending them to me. He said he understood and agreed to stop sending them.

He then shared with me he remembered how it all started with the molestation. He said, "It's neither here nor there," which was a famous line he had used countless times over the years. He said my sister had left us for the summer and had talked with me about "sex" and I was curious enough to come and start asking him questions at first. He said then, one day, I just came right out and asked him to see "it". Again, I was in disbelief. He continued on, saying he should have been strong enough to do the right thing, but he didn't, and he showed it to me, and things escalated from there. He quickly tried to recant, stating I wasn't to blame and he was the adult in the situation, and I was over the conversation at this point.

That was not how it happened. I remembered exactly how it happened initially, but it wasn't worth the argument for me because whatever he had to tell himself to sleep good at night wasn't my burden to carry. What I had learned in that moment was that there had been no sincerity in the apologies over the years. There was no true ownership or accountability taken by either of my parents. It was enlightening to hear this come out of his mouth to me as if I had not been there, experiencing it all those years.

The dynamics of the conversation changed when he shared with me he had recently, on the Thursday prior (July 22, 2021), attempted to commit suicide. He went into great detail about how he was driving home and drove around the back of the house, and pulled the gun from the holster. He said he closed his eyes and pulled the trigger, but the Holy Spirit came down and saved him. He said the Spirit said I changeth not, and if you do this, you will go to hell. He said the Holy Spirit told him he will have to go through it, but everything will be OK. He said he knew at the end of the day that things would work out the way they were supposed to.

He immediately assured me he had things under control and that my mother already knew about the incident, and he didn't need me to be concerned or call the pastor or notify my siblings. He was so sure that he knew it would never happen again. I remember thinking it felt like another manipulation tactic to try to keep me contained and in line, so the church people didn't find out.

I stared at him with a blank stare and told him my only concern was understanding how this impacted other family members and I hoped that he and my mom could focus on how to really fix the broken relationships between all of us.

He was enraged that I didn't respond how he expected me to about the suicide attempt. He said he was about to take his life because he beat himself up over and over about this. At the end of the day, he realized that nobody on Earth had a heaven or hell to put him in so he couldn't worry about it anymore.

He said the Holy Spirit also showed him that this thing was bigger than us and that I would share this testimony with millions of people because it was a part of my purpose. He said during that time, I would see that when other women shared their testimony, some had it way worse than I did.

He said, "Their fathers put it in their butt and forced themselves on them and we did everything but that." My face changed. My heart was in true disbelief. I was disgusted. The look in his eyes told me everything I needed to know about what I needed to do next.

He saw my face and immediately tried to clean it up by saying he wasn't trying to minimize what happened to me. In my mind, that was exactly what I knew he was attempting to do, but I wasn't having it. He advised that he understood I needed time and that he would always be there, no matter how much time lapsed. Even if it had been months since we had spoken, if I needed something and called him, he would pick up and there would be no love lost. He told me one day when he was gone, I would appreciate some things he had said over the years.

I asked him if he had ever molested or done anything inappropriate to my sister?

He replied immediately, saying, "No, never. I swear on my life." He shared one story with me and told me that if she ever told me anything different, she was lying.

He shared with me that my mom and I were the only two females in his life who ever showed him love. He explained he believed we would come out on the other side of this because the one thing we had on our side was God. Before he left, he looked me in my eyes and told me, "You better know hell will hit your household."

There was an eerie feeling that came over me, but I was quickly reminded that I was a child of God, daughter of the Most High, drenched in the blood of Jesus Christ! There was nothing that caught my God by surprise, to include this discussion, so I rebuked him in the name of Jesus.

The conversation ended, and he made a joke as he went to get back in his truck. I walked back to my safe haven as I closed my garage door behind me.

I was glad that was over. I wasn't the same little girl they could EASILY manipulate anymore. I was able to see them for who they really were and was able to determine what was best for me.

It was after this conversation that I realized I needed some serious intervention. If I was going to press forward with determination to stop letting my past control me, I needed professional help.

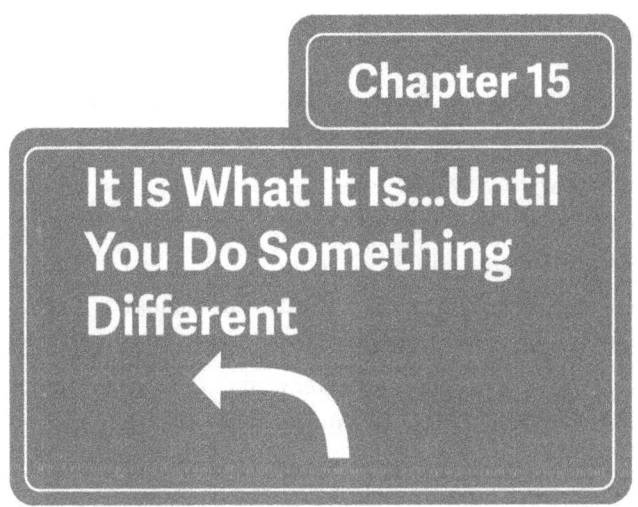

Chapter 15

It Is What It Is...Until You Do Something Different

I found myself in a panic and desperately scrolling my phone for counselors, therapists, psychiatrists—anybody who was a neutral third-party professional who could help me! I was done with the "Fake it Until I Make It" approach. I was sick and tired of having my voice silenced and feeling stuck in every aspect of my life. I needed someone who was totally disconnected from the situation and would be able to look in from the outside. I needed assistance, and quick, if I was going to continue to navigate this chaotic crisis of a life I was living.

It was a short process to lock in a licensed professional once I understood my options. Amid my desperation, I could not worry about the gender of the therapist or anything else, I just remembered praying to God that He assign someone who would be patient, proficient, and persistent through this journey with me.

Once a professional was assigned to me, I learned it would be a male and immediately felt a rush of uncertainty. My mind raced with all the things that could go wrong and focused on the reasons it may never work. I remember thinking a male would never understand. Nonetheless, I prayed and moved forward, despite myself. For once, I knew I needed to get out of my own way.

A lot of questions filled my mind the closer I got to the initial session, such as: *What will I say? How much of my life should I share with a complete stranger? What if they know my parents? What if the therapist reports it? Am I really ready for this?*

Here we were, July 30, 2021, and I received a phone call. I was reluctant to answer, but I picked up because it was my first session with my therapist. The session started off with him getting my name and confirming the details submitted. He explained that this initial meeting was set for thirty to forty-five minutes and was more of an intake session. We talked through what I hoped to get from the therapy sessions at the end of it all. I answered all the questions and we checked all the boxes. I briefly explained what had driven me to therapy and answered more questions prior to us ending the call. A sigh of relief was all I could let out after realizing this was a step in what I could only hope and pray was the right direction.

Over the next few days, I focused my attention on unpacking the initial call with my therapist. I left the call with some additional questions. I had been assigned to a male and wondered if he would be capable of really understanding the depths of my pain. I wanted to feel secure in that I was not opening up to just another person about my past, ultimately walking away feeling empty inside with no guidance and no resolution. I wanted to feel better about my future by believing I didn't have to live the rest of my life full of anxiety. I really was curious what my therapist could say to make me feel better about my circumstances and the cards I had been dealt. What could he suggest I do that I had not done up to this point? Would the time and effort I spent in these sessions really have a positive impact to the bottom line when it was all said and done?

In my conversations with God, I expressed my concerns and prayed He led me through this, allowing me to be open and committed to the journey. I prayed for clarity and direction and decided to leave it at His feet.

I accepted the next appointment and proceeded with the normal day-to-day activities in the meantime.

Session 2: My phone rang, and I must be honest, I was looking forward to the phone call, although I did not know what to expect. He introduced himself and confirmed he was speaking with the right person. In this session, he set the tone for the call by explaining the format, and we recapped the last call, prior to picking up from that place.

He asked me to elaborate a bit more on some of the situations that led me to therapy. I started by explaining that I was pregnant and had a lot of different emotions and I needed help to process them.

I shared with him what happened to me with my biological father when I was younger. I was able to go into some details about the molestation and the fact that it happened for approximately seven years of my life. Things started out as my father explaining he wanted to teach me some things so that little boys couldn't take advantage of me. He had conversations with me, advising that it wasn't "hanky panky" and it needed to stay between us.

In a short span of time, he decided to show me his private part and explained that boys and girls had different parts. He reiterated the fact by touching my parts and showing me his. In time, he started rubbing on my breasts and kissing me in the mouth. One day, he pulled out his private part and stroked it in front of me until semen came out. He explained to me he did this to show me that the sperm was what could get me pregnant.

He would come into my room in the middle of the night and climb into my bed. At first, he would lay next to me and put his arms around me. Later, he pulled me on top of him when he got into my bed, shifting his private part to align with mine. He usually had his boxers on, and I had on nightclothes, and he would make a grinding motion. From there, he had me suck his private part and he licked my private parts countless times.

My therapist listened intently, not interrupting while I shared this with him. He empathized with the fact that I had to endure this sexual abuse from someone who was supposed to protect me. He wanted to know the dynamics of my household, to understand who all lived together. In providing that information, I explained I experienced these things at different times and multiple times a week for years. My brothers were typically out, playing with their friends or asleep. My mother was usually in the field as she was in the military, and other times, she would be upstairs, and he would call me to the basement or wait until she was asleep.

Time was almost up for the session. He thanked me for opening up and sharing these things with him, acknowledging that it couldn't be easy. He did want me to understand that none of what happened to me was my fault. He wanted me to really take that in and believe that. He advised me he would send another appointment for our next session. I thanked him for listening and advised him I just wanted to heal for real. He said he understood prior to us ending the call.

My afterthoughts were a mixture. I appreciated the opportunity to talk through my trauma with a licensed professional. I believed there was hope for my healing after all. I thought about his responses and the tone in his voice as I shared all this information with him. I didn't know what I was expecting his response to be, but it wasn't shocking or over dramatic. He seemed to be in control and not a lot of reflection one way or another in his responses. It felt weird unpacking all the "family secrets", but this was my truth, and I needed help. I thought back on the few things he had said regarding none of it being my fault. I needed to not only hear that, but I needed to believe that.

I had a lot more to say and looked forward to the next session.

Session 3: We jumped right in after the usual formal introductions and confirmation he was speaking with the right person. He asked about my well-being and how I felt now that we had been in a couple of sessions and talked through some things that had contributed to me deciding to see a therapist. I told him I felt a little better, being able to share it with a neutral person outside of my friend circle. I wanted to know what I needed to work on and how to best navigate my complicated circumstance. He said he thought that was fair. We picked up from the last session, but he wanted to know what the current status was for my family dynamics with my parents, regarding how regularly we communicated with each other. I explained things had just gotten a bit more complicated before I decided to seek therapy.

I advised him that prior to what I was about to share with him, the communication had been regular, and we had been driving across town occasionally to spend time with them.

However, there had been a Fourth of July celebration that we had every year in different places that was at my parents' house this year. During that celebration, I had conversations with a family member who had brought up the sexual abuse I had encountered as a child. In this conversation, I learned that there were multiple family members who were not OK with what happened and had made a choice to not engage with my parents due to what transpired. Additionally, they advised me of some impacts and effects it had on the way they interacted with people and a big reason they struggled in relationships. They expressed how proud of me they were at how successful I had turned out to be, despite what happened. They cried, which made me cry and it stirred up raw feelings within me.

I knew what happened to me was not ideal and was wrong. I had gotten to a point in my life where I didn't want to make waves, but I wasn't willing to sacrifice my kids, either, so I pulled back from meeting up in person with my parents and focused on my family. I expressed to the family member that I had redirected my path to healing, by any means necessary, and was determined to break the cycle and generational curse. I am happy to be able to take a stand and say that it stops with me.

However, it broke my heart to know that others had also been impacted by what happened to me. I prayed we could all find some kind of peace and heal for real so we could move forward, whatever that looked like for each of us.

The family member advised they had enough of the "secrets" and felt a conversation needed to happen with my parents about it. I immediately explained that I didn't feel like any additional conversations were due to them on my part because, little did they know, I'd already had the conversations with my parents I felt were necessary. I encouraged them to have whatever conversations they needed to have to move on, but I didn't want to be drawn back into it, especially being pregnant. I was only trying to focus on not stressing out and getting through the rest of my pregnancy with a happy, healthy baby.

The family member advised they understood, but felt they had let me down because of how things were handled, and they felt terrible because they should have done more. I assured them I held no ill will toward how things played out because the choice they made to do something saved my life. It made a difference and I felt they did what was within their ability to do at the time and that was all I could have asked for. I told them to not harbor anything of that nature because I was forever thankful for the people who tried to do something, despite the result not panning out the way we felt it should. They were thankful to hear this and advised they felt it necessary to have some additional conversations with other family members and they would handle it as they saw fit.

We went our separate ways and I wobbled straight to the bed because it was the wee hours of the morning before I knew it. I found it hard to really relax after the discussion because my mind was in overdrive. A phone call happened between the family member and another, and we were advised of some additional breathtaking information that I won't share since it was not my story to tell.

With this new information, I was taken aback and decided that the extent of the abuse was deeper than I had known. It made me think long and hard about what my next move needed to be. A few more conversations had been had with other family members who knew of the situation, but not of the granular details of everything that transpired. With this information, the other party reached out to me and advised that a "sit down" needed to happen and they would like for me to be there to mitigate deflection and drama, but left it up to me whether I wanted to attend. I prayed about it, and we slept on it for some time prior to making sure we were not reacting on raw emotions.

Ultimately, we agreed the sit down with my mom was necessary and that entire conversation was relayed to my therapist.

He asked, "What happened next?"

I advised him after walking away from my mom, I felt there was only one thing left to do after she advised us she was not going to have the conversation with my dad about what we shared with her. She felt like it was not her place to have the conversation with my dad. The other party did not feel as they owed my father a conversation, but I agreed to do it because there were some things I needed to get out so I could move on.

From there, I prayed to God to order my steps and give me the strength to talk with my dad. It led me to "The Stand Up" in my driveway, seven months pregnant, facing him and expressing how what he had done to me impacted my life well beyond the abuse. I needed him to know what he did was wrong, and although I forgave him, it had contributed to the way I dealt with my husband, impacted the way I raised my kids, and had everlasting triggers I needed to heal from.

We walked away understanding that I was taking some time to focus on my healing and didn't want him texting me daily. My dad agreed to give me some time. There were a lot of things said by my father that day that did not sit well with me.

As I walked back to enter my house, I did not know that would be the last conversation we would have to this day. He thanked me via text for the talk and I advised him it was what was necessary so we could all find the way ahead.

The next day, he did not text me, which was a sigh of relief for me. The very next day, he did text me, and then called and left a voicemail, stating he knew I didn't want the text messages, but he just had to send them, and I didn't have to respond if I didn't want to. It was at that very moment I became irritated on a new level. It reminded me of how I was forced to feel as a child, like he was going to do what he wanted, despite what I wanted. It became very clear to me that he did not respect my boundaries. I decided to block him because I was tired of not having control of my own life, always having to take whatever people wanted to give me. I never looked back.

I wondered if I had overreacted or if I was wrong but my therapist reassured me it was important to set boundaries because it was how we showed others how to treat us. Through listening to me during our session, my therapist was able to detect that I didn't have any clear set boundaries, which left the door wide open for people to do what they wanted, how they wanted, when they wanted, which was not healthy for my mental state. We discussed boundaries were needed with my parents, but also in other areas of my life, and went over what that might look like moving forward.

Additionally, he challenged me to think about what I really wanted to accomplish at the end of the time we spent together. I expressed very clearly that I wanted to heal so my family could experience the best parts of me before I left this world. With that, he explained I needed to make a choice and consider being committed to changing the environment. He further elaborated that it was really hard to heal when you were operating in dysfunction. By going into their environment and signing up for therapy, it might cause some interference with the healing process, especially if I have troubles separating it. After some consideration, I agreed with this and committed to staying in my own household to focus fully on healing.

The session ended, and we confirmed that weekly sessions were working for me.

In the next couple sessions, we focused on the impact these childhood issues had on my family, within my household, and how it had affected the relationship with my mother.

For once in my life, I shared things with my therapist I hadn't ever spoken to anyone else about. I was being honest with myself that my trust in people was not very strong. I felt as though no man would ever be able to love me from the inside out and respect me. It was something I had carried for a long time with me over the years and I think it allowed me to settle.

Specific to my marriage, I found I struggled to enjoy simple things, such as being able to indulge in kissing my husband and enjoying deeper levels within our marital sex life. I wanted to give him more and be happy doing it, but something as simple as the thought would alter my mood or make me emotional. I had pushed myself occasionally and cried silently through it once and actually got physically sick in another instance. He was very understanding and assuring that it was OK and not something that was a big deal. To me, I just wasn't sure how to overcome it and felt I was letting him down because I wasn't able to fulfill my duties as a wife. It was easier for me to shut that part of me down than to try to deal with it.

I advised my therapist that I had to have a conversation with my kids at a very early age about good touch and bad touch. I showed my kids how to bathe themselves at an early age. I went the extra mile to try to have a relationship with my daughter, trying to overcompensate for what I felt like my relationship with my mom lacked.

With my older son, I had distanced myself from him unknowingly over the years. I couldn't hug on him for long periods of time or cuddle watching TV for fear of causing him to be uncomfortable. In my mind, I was so intentional about not inflicting the same kind of trauma onto my kids and I wanted a clear conscience. However, it caused a divide and I realized he eventually stopped seeking me for nurturing and would just go to his dad. That was when I noticed a difference and started paying attention to what was happening.

I felt my life taking a wrong turn because I didn't want him to feel neglected or abandoned in that area of his life. At the same time, I was damaged goods and didn't know how to reel it back in and find the balance. It brought tears to my eyes at the thought of it because that wasn't my intent, but here it was, my past coming back up, trying to rob me of my future.

I further expressed my desperation in trying to figure it out because, here I was, pregnant with another son, and I didn't want the same experience for him. I needed to figure it out, and quick.

My therapist empathized with me and said he could see how these different areas of my life could be impacted based on my childhood trauma. He explained that these thoughts and emotions were known as triggers that come from what I had been through. He explained he couldn't promise me that triggers would ever be fully eliminated or nonexistent. However, he believed that once we acknowledged them as triggers, the goal was to not be enticed by them and get to a point that they didn't control me or alter my mood the way they had up to this point. He explained it took time, but this could be accomplished, and he felt confident I could overcome and get to a better place with them.

During a session, he asked if I had ever been diagnosed with PTSD and I explained I had not. I further explained that I'd never spoken with any doctors and only one marriage counselor prior to speaking with him. He explained that the symptoms and the way I answered the questions pointed to PTSD and asked if I ever struggled with anxiety. I confirmed I had a season where I had. I was prescribed medicine and had to take it often initially, but prayed to God to heal me in this area, as I didn't want to get addicted to any medicine. I slowly got to a place where I only needed to take the medicine occasionally when my chest got really tight, and I couldn't control it and breathe through it.

I had regained control for a while and had only recently started having anxiety attacks when I got pregnant and was dealing with my parents and family members, pertaining to this childhood trauma conversation. I explained that this wasn't the only thing that caused my anxiety levels to be high. He inquired about what else was contributing to this condition and I mentioned the death of our first-born son, Braylen.

Being pregnant but remembering what happened during that pregnancy kept coming to my mind. I knew it was a coping mechanism to keep me grounded to prepare for the worst-case scenario. Losing my first-born son shattered my heart into a million pieces and was the biggest testimony I had. I didn't think I would make it through that, and GOD was the only way I made it through. I was forever grateful that God kept His hands on and over my life.

My therapist explained to me it was important to acknowledge what happened in the past while not allowing it to rob me of what was real in this moment. He helped me to understand that it was OK to acknowledge what happened in the past and be aware. However, it was just as important to live in the moment and appreciate what I had in front of me. Often, we lose sight of what's right in front of us by getting caught up in the past and what's behind us.

He stressed the importance of recognizing that this was how we got robbed of enjoying where we were in life right now. The truth was, I had an angel watching over us and God had blessed us with two more children, and one on the way. The hope was that we knew that if God brought you to it, then He will bring you through it. He blessed us repeatedly and I must believe to receive that He can and will do it again! I agreed and told him I would hold on to that. My faith had carried me to this point, and I just had to keep holding on to it.

The enemy comes to kill, steal, and destroy, and I couldn't let him rob me of this last pregnancy. He assured me it was OK for me to enjoy this pregnancy for what it was. I agreed and told him that despite me bringing this up in this session, I had been intentional about enjoying the pregnancy, especially since this was the last baby I was having.

The next few sessions were the same format and content. We always covered what was "new" from one week to the next. Then, he would pull up his notes from the prior session and we would work through it from there. My good news during that week was that I'd scheduled 4D pictures and a pregnancy photo shoot, and he was happy to hear it.

We went through the flow of me updating him on my home life and how things were going with a couple of steps I had agreed to take to try to embrace the healing journey. I told him I started being intentional about proactively loving on my son and getting out of my own head. I gave myself permission to love my kids the way they deserve to be loved. I was committed to *not* allowing my past to rob me of my future. I knew it wouldn't be easy, but I believed it would be worth it.

He asked me about contact with my mom and how things were going on that front. She had not physically been my way and the phone calls had been limited. When my mom would reach out, she made statements about coming to visit and would not show up. No courtesy phone call or text to advise she wasn't coming or anything, either. This became a routine and the expectation.

I expressed my frustration but told him I was working to reroute my energy to focus on the people and things that deserved it. As hurtful as it was, the state of our relationship was the way it was, and I couldn't continue to be stressed out about it, week after week.

My therapist asked me if I had shared with my mom the way I felt about her not honoring her visitation plans or the lack of phone calls and I told him no because I honestly felt she was grown and aware that she had grandchildren. It wasn't my responsibility to follow up with her or express my dissatisfaction with her choices pertaining to the dynamics of the relationship. One thing he reminded me of was that in this new phase, we don't make assumptions and suggested that I vocally express to her what I was feeling and see if things got better. He said we want to make sure the communication is clear so if we need to adjust avenues, we can, knowing that I was not operating in silence as I had before. He reminded me that this was the old Shae and not how we were moving going forward. He reminded me that the importance of changing the suffering in silence mindset was to challenge me to speak up. It may be uncomfortable or seem like it wasn't going to change anything, but time and actions would be the true tell of that.

Time had passed and she had not contacted us, so there wasn't much to update. I had withdrawn and decided not to call her either and embrace my peace.

Over the sessions, we had slowly been chipping away at the bricks that were built on a flawed foundation. Now, the new task was for me to rebuild my house on a firmer foundation with the values and principles I wanted to instill in my kids. I was excited to do this because this was the true testimony that God would get ALL the glory from!

I explained to him that the things that upset me to my core was how much my parents encouraged us to tell the truth, despite the consequences, and how family was over everything. The principles and values they pressed on and in us, I realized they didn't have themselves. That was heartbreaking to me. There were plenty of chances throughout the process where they could have owned the part they played and taken accountability so we could move forward. This had never happened.

Above everything else, I was most hurt at the way my relationship with my mom was. It wasn't the way I would have wanted it to end up, but what could I do? Through therapy, I learned we cannot change people and we shouldn't exert all our energy trying to. Instead, we should take accountability for the things we are supposed to and leave the other items for people to do the same. Sometimes, we must make peace with a situation, understanding we did everything we could, and we may never get an apology. They may never take accountability and always play the victim. That's their business and we can't make it ours. We can only make the choice to create and enforce boundaries as we walk in our victory that we have in Jesus Christ.

What my therapist explained he heard in my words was that I was hurt and there was no accountability or sincere apologies for all I endured, which made it hard to move forward. He explained that these two components were important for my mother and my relationship to possibly tread in the right direction. It was hard feeling like there was a genuine effort on her part to try to empathize with what I went through, acknowledge that she failed to make the right decision by staying with him, which contributed to the way our relationship was now. I confirmed that those missing components had been a blockage in the process for me.

I further explained to him that I used to always think the phrase "it is what it is" was as good as it got for my situation. I would say it so much, I really believed it. If they were my parents and were supposed to protect me and failed to do this, who else's responsibility was it? Who was going to save me? The simple answer always came back to me as *no one*. So, I was on my own to figure out how I was going to survive. I had to tuck it away in a deep place and try my best to forget about it.

The older I got, the more agitated I became with the phrase. I wanted to know what followed that statement. Was I supposed to just accept the way things played out? Continue to pretend it didn't happen to me and pray it didn't happen to my kids? The simple answer for me was, "I can't and I won't."

My new mindset was, "It is what it is…until you do something different." So, in that spirit, I was the difference that I wanted to see in my family, ultimately contributing to a bigger cause, breaking generational curses, so my kids had a chance in this world.

My purpose was bigger than me and the fact that God could use me to bless many more lives was mind blowing. The way I would press forward was by introducing the Long Handle Spoon approach, which allowed me to deal with people accordingly and unapologetically.

The Long Handle Spoon Approach was when I chose to deal with people at a distance when my boundaries were not respected. The idea was that I wasn't going to miss out on my blessings that God had for me for being too wrapped up in people's games and foolishness. So, the long handle spoon allowed me to keep people at a safe distance and still feed them, even if it was at another table. They didn't have to eat at mine if that didn't work, and as long as they ate, what was the issue?

Before we knew it, time was up again, and we were wrapping the call with the expectation that he would set the next appointment.

I was getting really close to my delivery date for Baby Justus and I needed to plan for his arrival. I reached out to a relative who lived out of state to see if they would be able to watch my other two kids while I was in delivery and recovery for a couple of days. They had circled back to me, confirming they would be able to assist us. My honest reason for doing that was to protect my kids at all costs. There was no way I was going to be comfortable leaving my kids with my parents, knowing what happened to me as a child.

My mom and I were not talking as much during this time, anyway, so I did not feel it necessary to let her know.

Sometime later, but prior to the delivery of Baby Justus, she reached out to me. I let her know that I had reached out to the family member to come and watch my kids while I was at the hospital. She was evidently upset about it but said they were my kids and whatever I wanted to do, it is what it is, before disconnecting the call.

She followed this up with a text message that said she didn't know why I was so bent on hurting her, but it is what it is. I messaged her back, explaining hurting her was not the intent, but I had to protect my kids.

Once again, I looked at the calendar, trying to speed up the time for my therapy session.

When the phone rang, I was eager to answer. We greeted one another and jumped straight in. He asked me how I had been since our last time talking and I advised him things were a little tense but controlled. Since it was closer to having my son, I had to make arrangements with a family member out of state to come in and help me out. I further explained that when my mom and I finally connected, I let her know and she was not happy and felt some kind of way about it. I explained our interactions via phone call and text.

He asked how I felt about the way things were. I told him I understood why she was upset, but I had to do what I had to do in order to protect my kids. I wouldn't apologize for that.

He asked if we had spoken since the exchange, and I told him we had very briefly. All of this was a part of the process, was what he explained. At times, there would be difficult decisions I would have to make, but the goal I needed to keep in mind was not to compromise my boundaries. At the end of the day, people would not always agree with the boundaries I set for myself and my family, and that was OK.

We spoke about some feelings that had surfaced because, for whatever reason, I blamed myself to some degree, regarding what happened to me as a child. When I dug deeper, I realized it stemmed from me wishing I had the strength to speak up sooner. I believed that due to the way things played out, my mother blamed me as well and it showed in the way she'd interacted with me since then. He did his best to reassure me I was a child and should not blame myself in any way regarding what happened. That was a part I would need to let go of because it was a part that just was and we couldn't change it. It was normal in these kinds of traumatic situations to not feel comfortable speaking up for fear of what else may happen, especially when there was a feeling no one was in your corner. He again reiterated for me not to take on the burden of blame and shame, but recognized it was easier said than done.

My doctor's office had placed me on bed rest due to having contractions. He encouraged me to focus my energy on our little bundle of joy who would arrive soon and get as much sleep as I could between now and then.

I had our healthy baby boy (Justus) in September 2021 and we agreed to schedule sessions after his birth after I had time to get settled in at home.

OCTOBER 2021 - DEC 2021 SESSIONS:

When the sessions picked back up, we spoke about life after Baby Justus's arrival. I remember being exhausted and drained for most of the sessions, but happy to pick them back up. He asked how home life was going with the adjustment of a newborn baby. We spoke about how exciting it was to have him finally here in our arms and how my kids had adjusted very well. We talked about my return to work being the next big hurdle I would have to address. I was a little anxious about what to expect in meetings and how the baby would be but digressed, advising one hurdle at a time.

My therapist encouraged me to focus on the excitement of having Baby Justus out of the womb, happy and healthy! I agreed to definitely embrace this. He asked if my mom had been to see the baby yet, and at that point, she had not. It had been a couple of phone calls and promises to come by, followed by excuses on why she wasn't able to make it.

She had sent a text message advising she felt like she was letting me and the kids down, but things were just really busy for her. We had not been speaking on the phone often, so I didn't really address anything and had been focusing on getting sleep and caring for my children.

Much of the sessions were focused on creating healthy, positive vibes and enjoying the time off from work with our baby. As the time got closer for me to return to work, it got really interesting. I was trying to find a routine and figure out a schedule that would work when Hubby went back to work. There were some frustrations and kinks we had to work through, and my therapist helped me to understand I needed to create boundaries in my home life as well. I needed to be vocal about assistance that was needed to avoid getting burned out at home and at work. I agreed to taking accountability and adjust accordingly to ensure my mental state was kept front and center.

My therapist advised me that he was going to bring up a topic that was going to be tough, but we needed to talk about it. He knew my beliefs and advised that we needed to talk about what reconciliation might look like with my father. I immediately felt a heavy feeling in my chest and had to be very honest with my therapist that I was not there yet. I wouldn't say I would never reconcile, but I needed time to really process everything that happened and focus on healing completely. He understood, but wanted to bring it up so we could start entertaining what this would look like and how the transition would look. At that time, I couldn't envision it, but I would remain open to it if God told me that was what I needed to do. Until then, the goal of healing for real was my focus.

While on the subject of reconciliation, I wanted to know if forgiveness was connected to allowing people to have continued access to you. That was what I had been raised to believe, but he said he did not believe the two had to be associated with each other. Forgiveness was a goal we needed to focus on, however, whether the access comes or not. I 100 percent agreed with that.

My conflict was that, through my journey, if I determined it was dysfunctional to try to go back into that environment, exposing my kids to him, was I wrong to forgive him but give him no access? That was a bridge we would cross when we got there, but it was something to consider in the meantime.

Our session ended, and we acknowledged we would talk again soon.

JANUARY 2022:

I was happy about the new year and looking forward to everything this year had to offer. At one of the first sessions of the year, I shared with my therapist that my motto was "Bet on YOU in 2022!" I explained how excited I was about this motto because it meant a lot to me that I made a choice and had invested in healing ME. I had been consistent in this choice, and it had shown to be fruitful. Although not where I ultimately wanted to be, I was making progress one session at a time. It meant a lot to me because I was dedicated to investing in my well-being, mental health, and healing journey. It was one of the best decisions I had made in my life.

I was focused on rolling the D.I.C.E on ME! The D was for dedicated. The I was for inspiring. C was for consistent. E was for empowering! Those were my core values, and with those being the foundation, it was bound to be firm.

I mentioned the long handle spoon again because I told him I realized I may have to pull it out of the toolbox and put it to use if people didn't change. He challenged me to sit my mother down and talk to her and be very clear in my expectations as we navigated moving ahead. I agreed to do this.

We talked about some things going on at work regarding my career path and I was in a good place there and at home. He had given me my assignment, so we wrapped up the call and wished each other well until the next session.

In between this session and the next one, I had a serious tug in my spirit. We had siblings who lived outside the house who did not know what happened within the household we grew up in. I battled back and forth with myself and even with some other family members on what the right thing to do was. At the end of the day, when I looked at it from their perspective, would I want to know something like this so I could make an informative decision if my kids wanted to visit or stay for summers? The answer was absolutely. I believed that was the right thing to do. I didn't know how it would be received, but I had a strong unction that wouldn't let me shake it off. I told God that I was not going to be like them and hold on to secrets that could be life changing for another child.

Once I shared the details, whatever relationship they chose to have and choices they made would not be on my conscience. What I did not want to happen was one of their kids have this happen to them and I have a hard time living with myself for not saying anything.

I made the choice to stand up and say something. I called the sibling and advised that I had something to share with them that would be hard to process, but I needed to be obedient and clear my conscience. We then had the conversation and I shared with them what happened when I was younger with our father and answered questions they had. From the response, I knew it wasn't their first time hearing it. They eventually shared with me that my dad had already called them to tell them about it, but the narrative was not the same. They stated our father had told them he woke up to me pulling out and sucking his private part and he should have stopped it as the adult but didn't. This information really changed the dynamics of everything that was a possibility in the future as it pertained to reconciliation between me and my father. It was at that moment, I realized he was willing to continue to humiliate me and drag my character up and through the mud. This escalated things to a new level because it confirmed that he was not truly sorry for what he had done to me. He was willing to continue to lie and manipulate to try to make himself not look so bad.

All I could muster the energy to say was that it was not true and that was not what happened, but whatever he had to tell himself to sleep at night was not my problem. I let them know I had blocked him some months back, and at this point, didn't think I would ever unblock him. It was shameful. It was hard to listen to the narrative he was trying to spin, and it made me sick, as if I had not been through enough.

They wanted to know why I was just sharing this when we had been in contact for years. I explained it was my truth and was not an easy conversation to have, but I was at a point in my life that I must release myself and was determined not to be like them with keeping secrets. I advised them that the conversation was not to change the dynamics of their relationship in any way, I just wanted to walk in my freedom.

They didn't appreciate the information being shared voluntarily, and then it being a lie, and said they confronted my father about the story via a group text to get to the bottom of it. I wasn't interested in the response and told them as much. My only concern was being obedient to what I felt called to do.

After that call with my sibling, I was in my feelings about the fact that my father was still the same person. The truth of the matter was, I knew it wasn't an easy conversation to have with anyone, but own what you did. It was hard to take him seriously, especially being all up in church, trying to share God's word, but living the complete opposite. I had no respect for him as a person and, honestly, no additional words left for him for the rest of my days.

My mind was in overdrive. I had decided I didn't want anything to do with my father anymore. It was best for me and my family. I had a small glimpse of hope that we could look into reconciliation one day if the time had come to do so. However, I had been ridiculed for the last time. I couldn't imagine what I could say to him at this point if I were to see him again.

Then, my mind jumped to my mother and all her inconsistencies and broken promises, and I was over it all. I knew her stance was we would have to deal with my dad in order to have a relationship with her. I didn't want to do it anymore. I shouldn't have to continue to be under this kind of scrutiny and I wasn't in the space to force relationships that were this hard to maintain.

She had so many excuses for why she couldn't come visit my kids for months at a time. She would agree to FaceTime the kids more regularly at a minimum, and it never materialized. I was disappointed but tired of having my heart broken repeatedly.

I had seen some pictures that other people had posted, showing she was hanging out and making time for other people, just not me and my kids. There were times my mom would share with me all the reasons she could not make it over to see the kids. However, if she knew her brothers were coming into town, she would make it her business to come over prior to them arriving. I couldn't help but to think that this behavior was intentional as it became a pattern for her. I was frustrated with the way things had been and it was overwhelming to try to think of people's intentions and heal at the same time. At the end of the day, we were not a priority for her, so I made the decision that we shouldn't be a choice for her. This way, she didn't have to feel obligated to choose.

I concluded it was easier to smile and hang with people who didn't know her deepest, darkest truth. That was fine, but I needed to heal for real, so I blocked her and deleted her off my social media pages.

To be honest, over the next few days, I didn't feel anything but free. I felt better knowing there were no expectations or broken promises lingering in the atmosphere. I had nothing to focus on except healing and my family. I felt good about my choice. I didn't feel like I owed her anything, and she didn't owe me anything either.

Some time went by before I received a phone call from my mom's home phone and business phone, which I ignored. One of my brothers reached out to me, saying Mom reached out to him, stating she thought I blocked her, and she had no idea why…

My therapist called my phone later.

February 2022 session:

I looked forward to this session more than my therapist would ever know. I had an update to share with him that changed how I viewed some things, and I needed some serious guidance. We jumped right in on this call.

He asked how I had been doing since our last session and if there were any updates with contact between my mother or father. My response to him was that I had an update, but I'd experienced some anxiety since our last session. He was shocked by this and asked what triggered it.

I told him about the pull I felt to call one of my siblings and share what happened to me as a child to clear my conscience and do things differently so I could be free. In doing this, I learned my father had already voluntarily contacted them, crying and telling them he had something to share with them, and if they didn't want anything else to do with him afterward, he understood.

He presented it as if he had wanted to share this with them for a long time and it had been eating at him over the years. He shared with them his version of what happened and then continued explaining what happened to him as a child. I was really upset by this news and couldn't process my emotions, but made sure to tell them that was not true.

Hearing he'd said those things, dug up a lot of emotions and left me feeling like I needed to take action. I was sick of the on-and-off relationship with my mom, the inconsistencies, broken promises and being an afterthought. I was tired. I had decided that there was no need to reconcile with my father and that meant the strain between my mother and me would remain. We were not a priority for her, and I decided to remove me and my kids from being a choice, so I blocked her, which led to one of my siblings calling me, upset, asking if I blocked our mom.

What I explained to him very bluntly was that I had blocked her because there was a right and wrong way to do things. He said that wasn't how we handled things and suggested I unblock her and reach out and explain why I had, but I rejected his suggestion. Instead, I told him I didn't owe her anything and I wanted to know where everyone was when I needed them because no one made any moves to protect me like they seemed to run to her rescue. Where were the conversations with her to advise how important it was for her to fix the broken relationships between her and her kids? Where was the accountability on her part? Everyone expected me to keep being the bigger person and take what people gave, and I was over it. We all had breaking points and I had reached mine. I was speechless at this point, tired of being jerked around, and I was setting boundaries that worked for me and my family.

So, she was blocked, and so was he. I was going to focus on healing so I could be the best version of myself for the family I had created. My kids deserved that.

My intent was to not unblock her until I felt I was in a better place and I was not sure how long that would take.

My parents were a package deal and would be treated as such. They both lacked accountability, and with the way things were, I wasn't able to truly focus on healing because of the distractions. Now, with both of them out of the picture, I could at least not expect anything from them and put my focus where it needed to be because my life was not a game. My struggles and pain were real, and healing mattered to me. No one would ever be able to understand the depths of my pain, no matter how much I cried and tried to put it into words.

Also, I told him my struggle was trying to get out of the manipulation cycle that came with dealing with certain people as that had been my experience. I explained it had been hard for me to try to unpack some of the reasons certain decisions were made and discern between genuineness and manipulation. The way the events were unfolding, honestly made me feel like I was part of a sick game I didn't want to play. I wanted to exit left and live out the rest of my days without dealing with the stress that came with my past. I wanted to heal.

My therapist listened very intently and reminded me we couldn't change people. He also explained that it could be stressful trying to unpack all these things, especially with so many people involved. He recommended I take control back and be OK with shutting conversations down with other family members when they called to try to unload on me. Unknowingly, that could be a contributing factor that added additional complications to an already complicated situation.

He encouraged me to take whatever time I needed to myself to take care of me and keep in mind the importance of not shutting myself out from being open to a genuine apology, should that attempt be made.

I had already done a lot of the hard work by having the difficult conversations with my parents over the years. He empathized with the fact that it couldn't be easy to do that, but now there were new challenges I was facing and it required action. The good news was that I was in control of what action, and he wanted me to know that I could always change avenues. I told him the action required at this time was me pulling out that long handle spoon. I needed to really think about some things.

Our session ended, but he wished me well and told me he was proud of me and trusted that I would continue to make good decisions. We discussed when the next session should be prior to ending the call.

About three weeks passed and there wasn't much of an update for me to share during my therapy session as I still had no contact with my mother. I was able to think much clearer and really focus on my family. I expressed I had no anxiety attacks during this timeframe and didn't have the cloud hanging over my head of the child sitting at the window, waiting for the absent parent to show up. I used that time to really think about how I could make sure my relationship with my kids were intentional and meaningful. While I understood there was no book to parenting, I believed we should make it a top priority to have healthy relationships and maintain them to the best of our ability. I was able to envision what I hoped my relationship with my kids would be in the years to come.

I spent a lot of time reflecting on the things I appreciated that my parents had instilled in us versus the interactions that were not ideal. I had a chance to really disconnect from all the distractions that had me in limbo from one week to the next. It was at this point I appreciated what my therapist had said in an earlier session. He explained it was possible to try to focus on healing while still be connected to the source of your pain, but very difficult to do. He challenged me to make that determination for myself and be willing to adjust as necessary. This was one of those times where I had to make a hard choice, but it was necessary to adjust to obtain the level of peace I expected to maintain.

This set the new standard for how I would prioritize my peace on purpose moving forward. Aside from this, the energy I was able to redirect helped me to imagine what the way ahead really looked like.

March 12, 2022 - There was a knock on my front door, which was out of the ordinary for us, outside of food deliveries, ever since Covid had started. I pulled out my phone to check the doorbell camera and saw my mom standing on my porch. It was a day before my thirty-fourth birthday. Here I was, at a crossroad again, faced with deciding I prayed I wouldn't regret. I said a quick prayer to ask God what I should do because, in all honesty, I didn't want to make the wrong move. I was just getting used to what seemed like my new normal. A couple thoughts went through my mind, and I heard my therapist's voice in my head, saying something along the lines of not being closed minded to the idea that they may very well have a time where they genuinely want to attempt to make it right.

With this thought, I made a promise to myself that no matter what was said, I was not going to be drug back into the cycle of manipulation. I took a deep breath and opened the front door.

She had a look on her face that was somber, and I couldn't even look at her for a long time. I had my baby on my hip and the tension was so thick, he started crying uncontrollably. I had never heard him cry like that before. My husband had to grab him and take him away. We stood by my front door, speechless for a short while. She reached out and hugged me and we just stood there a little while longer. In that moment, I honestly felt empty, numb, and like I had nothing to offer her. It was sad.

We made our way to the couch and sat down near each other in silence for a little longer. She reached over and put her arms around me and cried, rocking side to side.

She started off explaining that she was at a loss and tried to give me time because she didn't want to cross my boundaries. She said she prayed to God to lead her when the time was right to reach back out to me. She explained she wanted me to tell her whatever was on my mind and heart and don't worry about how it comes out. She said if I needed to scream, curse, or whatever, just please say something. The way our relationship was now, she was not OK with it and wanted to figure out how to get on a different path. She said she did not know why I blocked her, and she was very hurt when she discovered I had. She said she felt like I put her on the same level as my dad and that cut deep.

Tears rolled down my face and I stared into the distance.

I told her I was done trying to figure it out because it kept breaking my heart that our relationship was the way it was. I had high hopes that things would change, and we could somehow focus on what our future should look like, but it seemed impossible. I expressed my dissatisfaction with the fact that it felt like me and my kids were not a priority to her. I let her know I had seen photos of her on social media before I blocked her, showing up to other people's functions, but making excuses for why she couldn't visit us. I told her it hurt me that my kids would never have the grandparents they deserved. My kids didn't even ask about them and that was crazy. It was painful knowing I was her only daughter, and she didn't make a genuine effort to fix what was broken. I told her I had been crying out for years and she had not been listening. Now, I had to focus on healing and being the best version of myself for my family because they didn't deserve a broken version of me.

To her, she couldn't comprehend what I was saying because she believed we had a good relationship. She thought we were able to talk about anything and that we were in a good space. On the contrary, the dynamics of our relationship had been rocky for a long time.

She explained it had been hard with the way things were. She understood I was working on healing, but it had been tough for her, trying to find a balance between giving us time and my dad time without letting someone down. When I was pregnant, she was more understanding because she blamed the hormones, but things were still the same.

She explained that if she called me, she had to deal with him walking out of the room and feeling some kind of way. If she didn't show up at my house or call for a while, then she had to deal with the fact that she was letting us down. It had been really hard, and then the fact that she had her mom living with her added another layer of responsibilities.

It was important that I clarified it wasn't just about her failing to come over, but she didn't even bother to send a courtesy message to say she wouldn't be coming. It was the fact that she didn't even text or call on a regular and she broke promises repeatedly. It was the fact I felt we were an afterthought and her actions had shown we were not a priority to her. It was like if she had to make a choice to let someone down, it was going to be us every single time. That was the part that continued to break my heart, and I needed to be free from it.

Free from the disappointment I had grown accustomed to. In all the major tragic events of my life, she hadn't shown up for me. When I lost my son, I needed her and it was like she didn't know how to be there for me. Every pregnancy, I had to be on my own because she didn't want to get her hopes up in case something happened to the baby.

I had seen her show up for other people, so I knew she could do it, but it felt like she had chosen, for whatever reason, not to for me. It felt like the kid who had a parent who lived outside the home who promised they were going to show up, so the kid got all excited, packed their bag, and sat, staring out the window, waiting for them to show up.

Except, they didn't show up. Ever.

That was how I felt repeatedly, even though that was the one thing that had been consistent. Because of the love and hope in my heart, I kept showing up, only to be let down.

There comes a time in your life where you have to understand and accept things for what they are and not what you hope for, and adjust accordingly. I had been understanding of all things she had to do in order to try to balance her circumstances. Honestly, it was this way because of the choices that were made, so she had to figure out how to make it work because I didn't have that answer. I reminded her that at the beginning of the year, we both vowed to make a better effort to communicate with each other. When I felt like she was at least trying, I pushed myself, despite how it made me feel inside. But a part of my healing was accepting accountability for my part and leaving the parts that weren't on me in the lap of the other party. I realized I couldn't change people and that was not my intent. All I could do was set boundaries and enforce them so I could understand what was healthy and what was not.

The old ways of doing things weren't working for me. They were dysfunctional. I learned how to operate normally in a dysfunctional situation for a long time and had not even realized it. For me to heal for real, I must keep things that are not conducive to where I am headed, separated. I didn't know how long it would be for, but I was allowing God to lead me in that.

She apologized for the impact it had on me, although it was never her intention. In the time we had not been communicating, she was able to realize that intent did not matter; it was about how I was impacted. While she didn't like the way things were with her family, she understood it resulted from the decisions made. Understanding she couldn't force relationships, she vowed to not do that any longer. All she wanted to do was focus on the relationships that were still available to her, and she was willing to do whatever it took to show us that.

She acknowledged she had not been consistent or as committed as she had hoped to be. She said she honestly did not know that I felt some type of way about it because I seemed very understanding when she would come back around.

Just as I felt some kind of way about her not checking in for extended periods of time, she felt the same way as I had not been checking on my grandmother. She said she understood I had made a choice that worked for me, but with that choice, my grandmother felt the backlash when she had nothing to do with anything. She stated it was impacting everyone in some way and it was not easy to try to navigate it.

I agreed that nothing about what was happening was easy. However, when we said we wanted something different, we had to do something different. That required making choices that might make people uncomfortable. They might not agree, but I had to do what was best for me in this season of my life. I'd had many heart to hearts with my grandmother and she knew exactly how much I loved her and where we stood. I had to really make peace with the fact that she was indirectly impacted by a decision that I had to make now to come out better on the other side. I owned the fact that I could do a better job checking in on her, but the only way was through my mom, which was not an option when I redirected my focus and decided to block her. I also shared with her the details on how the blocking decision came about.

I told her I spoke with one of my other siblings who had not grown up in the household, knowing they brought their kids around and they should make informed decisions.

I was made aware that our dad had already reached out and shared his version, which was a lie, further humiliating and devastating to me. I shared the details that were told to me and explained to her I did not appreciate it, and I didn't want or need to deal with my father anymore. It wasn't healthy and I had no words for the continued hurt and pain he continued to inflict on me.

I let her know I was broken again because of that and us not making any progress in our relationship. Despite all that, I could honestly say I had forgiven both of them and loved them, just not the things that happened and the decisions that followed. I couldn't explain why or how, but I did because that was who God created me to be. I had to take a stand in my life for something or fall for anything.

More than anything, I wanted my parents to take accountability for the role they played in my brokenness. My mother said her only concern was focusing on the relationships with those who were willing to rebuild because she couldn't change the past. The past wasn't what I wanted to change. I simply wanted her to acknowledge and take accountability for failing to protect me as a child. That was the biggest hurdle preventing us from moving forward. I didn't feel there had been a sincere acknowledgment of the trauma inflicted on me and the impact it had on my life.

I never got any help or counseling growing up and neither did my father, which I felt, at minimum, should have happened prior to any next steps being discussed. Yes, she apologized, but it was always attached to something like, "I feel you feel I failed you, so I guess I failed you" or "I apologize you feel the way you do."

Ultimately, she wanted to know what needed to happen for us to move forward. She wanted me to promise to talk to her when I felt some kind of way should she start reverting to her old ways, instead of blocking her again. She expressed she loved me very much and I meant a lot to her.

I told her I loved her, too, and explained that I couldn't make a promise to talk to her, although I would try. We were both grown and when you wanted something, you were willing to work for it. We both knew when we were not doing what we were supposed to be doing. I should not be responsible for always holding you accountable. I agreed to hold myself accountable and suggested she do the same. I didn't want the empty promises of you coming over to see my kids if you are not going to show up.

She said she would do her best, but she couldn't make a

promise about coming over often but would definitely at least call and FaceTime more. She said to mitigate broken promises, she would reach out when she was in route and be sure she was able to come over.

We hugged each other, she saw the kids briefly, and we spoke about a new hobby my daughter and I had taken on called diamond painting. She requested we do this together to relax and bond. I told her this was fine.

She asked me to think about unblocking her so she could start calling again and I unblocked her phone calls, but she was still not friends with me on FB.

She thanked my husband on the way out to her car for loving and taking care of me in her absence.

Over the next few days, I reflected on the conversation, trying to compartmentalize my emotions. I learned I needed those three to three and a half weeks of silence and no distractions prior to her coming back around. I had finally gotten to a place in my life where I was open to seeing how things changed after the conversation, but I didn't become emotionally vested in it either way.

One thing I knew for sure was that time would absolutely expose the truth in people by their actions. She had shown me way too many times what was important to her, and she lacked consistency and follow through.

I honestly felt the gesture she had taken to come over was out of character, and I appreciated the effort. She put her pride to the side, so I was willing to give it a chance, and at the same time, protect my heart in the process. The break had allowed me to pull back enough to be OK either way. It was in that moment I learned, "It is what it is…until you do something different."

During my therapy session immediately following this discussion with my mom was where a shift happened. We discussed in detail the conversation she and I had. The therapist asked me to explain how I felt following the discussion. I was very honest in saying I must give her credit for putting her pride to the side and driving across town to sit down with me to have a heart to heart. I appreciated the fact that she allowed me to get a lot off my chest. There were parts of the discussion that still felt like there was still a struggle with accepting accountability, but I didn't know if I would ever see that day come with her.

I advised him I opened the door for her because I heard his voice in my head and I told him what it said. We laughed. I told him I realized how important it was to block her so I could take a break from all distractions, and it helped me to prioritize what's important to me. It allowed me to draw strength deeper within myself that I didn't know I had. It allowed me to disconnect for just enough time to not be as vulnerable as I was, but not as cold-hearted as I feel I was headed toward. It was a good place and space to be for me because while I was open to the change, should it be genuine and actually happen, I was not waiting around, twiddling my thumbs. I was happy to do my part, but I was not going to go any extra miles.

I told him it felt good to feel like she was present in the moment with me and not just checking off a box. It felt great to be honest and get it all out on the table because sometimes we reached a point where it was just easier to shut down. I learned some things as well that bothered her I was not aware of as it pertained to my grandmother. Ultimately, I shared with my therapist that I was going to see how things went and adjust however I saw fit.

My therapist applauded me for standing up and speaking out. He knew that had been a struggle and not an option in the past. He explained that that discussion, in his opinion, was long overdue. He added that a lot of relationships were ruined through miscommunication or misunderstanding.

Many times, things could have been resolved through a simple conversation. He said he wasn't sure that was the situation with us, but it was good to know that we had it. Now he said time would show if she was truly apologetic and if she wanted things to be different, then she would make a true effort to change it. If she at least made an honest attempt to fix the broken relationship with me and my kids, it would be impactful, and we could build on that, he believed. However, I needed to understand that there was always that possibility that people would fail to meet the expectations and promises made, especially long term.

He wanted me to be open to this being an outcome as to not be disappointed and revert backward when we had made some great progress over the last eight months. I advised him I was focused and dedicated to the end goal, which was to heal for real. With this, I reminded him I had my long handle spoon that stayed on the ready! We laughed again.

He expressed his excitement for the progress I had made and expressed that people like me were scarce. I was on the right path and just needed to keep the goal in mind. He assured me he was there and available for as long as I needed. I thanked him for his time, patience, and guidance as I navigated through this healing journey because it had not been easy and had been up and down, but very rewarding. I had him to thank for listening and showing up session after session, always ready to encourage and motivate me as well as redirect me when necessary.

Multiple sessions with my therapist transpired over the next few months and we continued to discuss what happened from the last time we met until the appointment the next week. The format was the same and the emotions ranged from one extreme to the next.

In our **May 2022 session**, we spoke about spreading the sessions out to bi-weekly instead of weekly for a couple months with a goal of getting to once a month with a personal goal to be therapy free heading in to 2023!

JUNE 2022 SESSION:

During this session, my therapist and I discussed how things had been going. I had an exhaustive day at work for multiple reasons, but to see this call come through changed the entire environment and trajectory of my day. I felt a burst of an amazing vibe fill my atmosphere. I had so much I wanted to share with him, and it felt like forever since the last session, but I had more than managed in between them.

I candidly shared that my mom had regressed to her old ways with the many reasons she couldn't make it over weekend after weekend to see me and my kids and had not been over in quite some time. He wanted to know how that made me feel, but it did not have the same impact it had on me previously. I didn't think twice about it and felt nonchalant when she canceled or went a week or two without calling. No anxiety. No bitterness. Not mad. Just done with placing my energy in the wrong people and expecting people to change because I wanted them to.

I'd accepted that she is who she is and I should not be forcing people to do anything they didn't want to do. If they didn't want to put in the effort or prioritize us, then why do we want them around? We don't.

Blocking her in February 2022 helped me really focus and place my energy where it mattered, understanding that she and I's relationship had been damaged for a very long time. I let him know it wasn't causing me any anxiety or heartache, to be honest. It didn't hurt the same way. He was happy to hear it and assured me that this was a good way to measure my growth and healing progress.

We spoke about other things I'd been up to and any other concerns or things I'd run into. I advised him that my dad was still blocked and had been for almost a year now, but he had messaged my husband on Father's Day. My husband let me know and I immediately felt anxiety try to kick in and I wanted to understand it. He explained to me from a psychological perspective there are some things that will always be triggers and I will learn how to cope and deal with them, but they may never completely go away.

He broke it down as two hands, and on one hand, this is a person who hurt me, abused me sexually, and took advantage of me. On the other hand, deep down, there's the fact that he is still my father, family, and my blood. So, the God in me on my faith walk still allows me to feel that as well. I understood it and we moved on.

I let him know that I'd prayed and decided it was time for me to start my book. It was connected to my purpose. What I had to say could help many people and he encouraged me to follow through as it would continue to help me and others who had been silenced. I was encouraged to be the voice for those people who were too scared to speak up but needed this to advance to their next season.

My testimony had the power to bless so many people on a personal and spiritual level, he told me, as I'd been an inspiration along this journey for him as well. I assured him I planned on it and discussed with him the new challenges I faced regarding what comes with that.

I understood my relationship with my mom would be forever changed. I understood people would read all the gritty details attached to my truth and testimony and would have a multitude of emotions and opinions attached. I explained even in understanding this, I'd talked to God about it, and I had His permission and assurance that it was bigger than me. He had already prepped me for what was to come at different seasons of my life and He would continue to be right there with me. He had confirmed that this was directly in line with my purpose.

A quote that popped in my mind was, "They say hurt people, hurt people. So, in my mind, that means healed people should help people." That was what I hoped to accomplish in sharing my truth. It was about being transparent and providing proof that God is who He says He is. If He did it for me, He will do it for you! If you believe He can, then He will, because I know how much God has done for me. I owe Him my life and some more. I could never repay Him, but the least I could do was fulfill the purpose that was connected to my life. There was purpose in the pain. It wasn't in vain.

He agreed and encouraged me to stay blessed and keep doing what I was doing. I thanked him for being persistent and on this journey for almost a year. He thanked me for being such an inspiration to him. We wished each other well until the next session.

JULY 2022 SESSION:

During this session, I celebrated the fact that I had officially been in therapy for one year! I was proud of myself for sticking it out and explained that sometimes we were moved by "feelings" and once we got what we needed, we thought we were good and at times fell off from the source that helped us to overcome the difficult times.

I wanted him to know that I was focused on counting my blessings and not my burdens. I was happy that I was able to see my growth and measure it through the difference in my physical and mental health. I told him I was not having anxiety nearly as much as I was prior to therapy. I could talk about what happened without getting really worked up. I acknowledge I experienced a traumatic childhood that ultimately led me to discovering the ultimate strength that is unleashing in my adulthood. I had no regrets. I knew we served an intentional God, and He used it all for the good. He saw me for who I was now and beyond what I went through back then. Nothing catches God by surprise, and I find solace in that fact. God already worked this out well before I could ever imagine being as healed as I am today.

He congratulated me on this milestone and assured me it was an accomplishment. I told him I didn't just show up session after session, but I did the work that was required for me to experience the change I wanted to see by making the choice to choose me and heal for real. He agreed.

We talked a little more about the book and my progress I was making on it. He wanted to make sure it was still a focus for me, and I told him absolutely. Lives would be changed, and people would have hope to break free, take a stand and speak out. It was important that I fulfill the purpose and help people.

We finished the session and scheduled for the next one.

I had a lot going on and missed the **August 2022 session**, but reached out and scheduled the next one for the following month.

SEPTEMBER 2022 SESSION:

September became a bit more interesting as I had gotten promoted, and I was still loving my career, although it was as demanding as my baby who was about to turn one already! I was excited and ready to learn more in my role, all while balancing my home life as a wife and mother. I became a little frustrated, which I thought came with working from home and always being inside for most of the time. I expressed this to my therapist, and he helped me walk through what my average day/week looked like. He expressed the importance in me maintaining a healthy work/life balance and prioritizing myself and what I needed just as much, if not more than, anything else. My eyes filled with tears because I felt guilty for what I was about to say, but it was something I felt was contributing to my mood change.

I was overwhelmed in all aspects of my life. I loved being a mother and it presented its own challenges, and I didn't really get a "break" or time to myself. He asked if I had expressed this to my husband and I told him to an extent, yes, but I felt guilty and put my needs to the side and trying to get some me time when they were asleep. That hadn't been working all that great because I was so mentally and physically exhausted by that time, all I wanted to do was go to sleep too. This led to the cycle starting over the next day and ultimately expanded into days, then weeks before I knew it.

He explained I shouldn't feel guilty about this because it was a shared responsibility, and encouraged me to think about what I needed and then express it to my husband. He encouraged me to make sure I was not just setting boundaries but also enforcing them in all areas of my life, which would ease some of the pressure.

In asking about my work schedule, I told him I didn't really hold myself to a schedule and more so focused on where I could cut the day off with no hot ticket items open. This had the potential to be problematic if it was not properly managed, was what he explained to me. I felt I had it under control, but he really stressed the importance of being able to step back and observe my boundaries and be willing to set new boundaries.

Sometimes, we can have lines in the sand that are clear to us but blurred or unclear to others. This causes unnecessary frustration, which could be resolved by re-evaluating my boundaries often enough to make sure they are clear. If it was blurry to me, then it wouldn't be clear to anyone else where my boundary is.

I thanked him for that feedback because I believed that was an area I still needed to work on. He then told me to commit to enforcing the new boundaries and stick with it to mitigate becoming too anxious and overwhelmed.

He wanted me to talk through what new boundaries looked like for my home life with my husband and my work life. I assured him that my job was very supportive and didn't require the kind of pressure I put on myself. He laughed.

I needed to try to disconnect at some point, and no matter what, not log back on to work once I was done for the day. I was warned that it would be hard initially, but it would eventually become a habit. I agreed to work on this, and he told me he was going to ask about it next time we met.

Also, he explained that as important as it was for others to take accountability, it was important that I, too, continued to grow and hold myself accountable. He expressed his excitement for my progress and being able to recognize some things that needed attention and assured me he knew I would work through them and be OK.

He asked me about my book, and I told him it was still coming along. I was not in a rush as I was on God's timing, so I was on time. He said he couldn't wait to read it because he believed I had some really great things to share and that it would change a lot of lives and help so many people who needed it. That was my prayer and my hope because it wasn't about me and I knew it was bigger than me.

I advised him I never considered writing a book, EVER, especially not about these hard things I'd experienced. I knew it would leave room for people's opinion and that part would be what it would be. The thing that pushed me was knowing this was a God thing and connected to my purpose, so I would be obedient and see it through. No matter how tough it got, this was my truth and I must believe that God brought me through it to reach back and help others who need to be motivated to make a choice to change.

I told him a big part of the book would be about some of these sessions because they honestly changed everything for me. I feel so free and in a much better place than I was over a year ago when I came to him. I told him I was scrambled, all over the place. I was having conversations and speaking up, but was still stuck and running around with no true guidance. Now, I could honestly say the veil had been lifted and I could see me the way God sees me and not how others do.

I was able to release the shame and guilt that became my baggage over the years. I could walk in my victory by holding myself accountable for the part I was responsible for. He helped me see that my part was to make a choice to heal for real and commit to the process and see it through.

In the lowest moments, he helped me see it from a new perspective, and at the same time, didn't dismiss my feelings. At the highest, he kept me grounded in understanding that seasons change, and nothing lasts forever. Enjoy it and know that challenges will still come. I was in control of not only setting boundaries, but also enforcing them. I was thankful for all the time spent. He assured me he had enjoyed the time and learned some things along the way from me.

We wished each other well until the next session, after confirming the next appointment should be the following month.

OCTOBER 2022 SESSION:

As it got closer to the session, I couldn't help but replay a prior conversation I had and wanted to talk through it with my therapist. In early October, my mom contacted me, and during a normal conversation, she mentioned my grandmother wanted to have a birthday party and requested they make her a big burger. They were having the get together at her house and all my uncles would be coming up to celebrate. I advised I would Cash App her some money to contribute to the celebration for my grandma after she mentioned wanting to order her a cake and getting her a nice dress. I sent her the money via Cash App after we wrapped up the conversation, which we agreed she would use to pay for my grandmother's cake.

My therapist wanted to know how I felt after that phone call. If I were being completely honest with myself, it was an overwhelmingly emotional feeling that rushed my entire body. I was torn because a BIG part of me wanted to celebrate my grandmother with my family. However, the other part had come so far and where I was in my healing journey, and the dynamics and boundaries I'd set with those relationships, wouldn't allow me to backtrack.

I had not spoken with my father in fifteen months, and being honest with myself, it wouldn't be respectful for me to show up at their house with us not being on speaking terms. Ultimately, I had to be real with myself and walk in my truth by standing by the choices I made. One thing I prided myself on was being able to live with the choices I'd made, be it good, bad, or indifferent. This consequence was directly related to the boundaries I had set. This was a true test of what truth I was willing to stand up in —mine or theirs.

Simply put, I knew what I needed to do, even if it went against what I wanted to do. Even though I knew what decision I had to make, that didn't stop the tears from welling up in my eyes and rolling down my face. They were warm as one after another trailed down my cheeks. My heart felt an ache I had not felt in some time now.

As the days grew closer to my grandma's birthday celebration, there was a tug of war going on internally. I asked myself, would it kill me to just pack my kids up and drive across town to my parents' house, putting things aside to celebrate my grandmother? Then again, I asked how it would impact the healing journey I'd been on and was I willing to risk it all for a couple hours? How would this really impact me if it set me back or threw me into an anxiety attack? Would I be obligated or expected to revert to the old way of doing things? I felt like, for once in my life, I was more in control of it than I'd ever been. I didn't want to lose that progress or gained ground for anything.

During the tug of war in my mind, it triggered me and led to me being upset. I allowed myself to feel it all in that moment instead of dismissing or deflecting. I recognized it for the painful moment it was and reminded myself I could not unpack or live there.

Looking in the mirror, I was reminded of the broken-hearted

young girl, who was in the middle of a healing battle she was determined to win. I thought about all the losses I had taken in my life and decided enough was enough. There was no better day than today to stand up and do what was best for me at this stage in my life.

The celebration happened for my grandma, and one of my uncle's birthday. The compromise was, in addition to paying for the cake, my mother would call me via FaceTime when they were about to sing Happy Birthday as a group. She did keep this promise, but unfortunately, I missed the call as I was asleep with my baby. I returned the call but did not get an answer.

My mother reached out sometime the next week. When I answered, she had a familiar tone that I recognized as her being irritated. She explained she was tired and didn't know what else to do. She said all this stuff going on was so overwhelming for her and hard to try to sort through.

She further elaborated that she never imagined our family dynamic would be the way it was and it was taking a toll on her. I assured her it wasn't easy for me, either, and she said all she could do was trust God. I agreed with that sentiment, but knew my priority was doing what was best for me and my family. I needed to focus on healing and I couldn't do that operating in a dysfunctional environment.

My mother continued to express that she understood where I was coming from, but she felt some type of way because none of her kids showed to celebrate her mother and her mother was innocent.

I told her I understood what she was saying, but it resulted from choices that had been made. There was a lot I had to consider, but it was a decision I made based on where I was in my healing journey at that time.

She shared with me she had a breakdown while my uncles were there and told them she had decided that she was hanging in there for my grandmother. However, when my grandmother passed, she planned on packing all her things up and leaving everyone behind. A fresh start somewhere she could live out the rest of her days the way she deserved to was what she sought.

I didn't have much to say except for, "If that's what you feel you have to do and what's best, then I get it."

My therapist wanted to know how this conversation made me feel and I was numb, honestly. Manipulation was a word I'd use to describe how certain things made me feel in different scenarios, and that conversation was yet another example.

I remember sitting on my bed and shaking my head as I heard brokenness in her voice. I told him I walked away, having to ultimately remind myself how far I had come on my healing journey. I had to come to terms with the fact that we all must cope and maneuver through this new normal. I knew it was important to respect my own boundaries and understand that everyone had a right to make decisions that were best for them. The truth was, I could see my mom going off and leaving everyone behind, but she wouldn't leave my dad.

The fact of the matter was, due to the dynamics of how our family was, it had raised questions that made her uncomfortable and she didn't want to face them. The old me would have considered how challenging this must be for her and think of a way to resolve it, which would mean sacrificing me and what I wanted to make them happy. However, the new and improved version of me, being the best me for my family, couldn't worry about how uncomfortable it was for them because my healing was more important. Honestly, it might be easier for them to move away so they didn't have to face people who knew the deepest, darkest secrets. It wasn't for me to figure out what was best for them or not. I had to continue to choose me and my family, and that was my focus.

I shared with him I was proud of myself during that conversation with her because I did not internalize her emotions and frustrations. I heard her and acknowledged the disappointment she felt in the choice we had made to not show up for a special event. I had experienced that same disappointment as I truly did not want to miss my grandmother's birthday celebration. I was proud that I did not revert to my old self and feel like I needed to over explain my reasons for my decision I made not to go. I had contributed financially and knew the way I felt about my grandmother in my heart and had expressed this to her when we last saw each other. I had to find peace in this and stand firm in the choice I made, understanding she did not agree or appreciate it.

My therapist acknowledged he felt I handled it nicely. He shared in my accomplishments and growth because it was a win, at the end of the day. He reminded me that when it came to boundaries, there would be more uncomfortable conversations that would transpire and encouraged me to stay strong and stand tall in the decisions I make.

I also explained that it felt like I had been sacrificed so many times in my life by my parents and I wasn't going to stand for it anymore. I had to tell her it hadn't been easy for me, but it was something I needed to do for me and my family. While she said she got it, that didn't mean it was comfortable or she agreed with it and that was her right to feel that way.

I knew this was all God because, in all honesty, I still loved my parents, despite what happened to me and the decisions that were made. I didn't harbor any hate in my heart, and I had forgiven them. What I learned, though, was that even though I forgave, that didn't mean I had to allow them to have access to me if I felt it was unhealthy for me or my family. That was my right.

I also understood that what happened to me as a child was not my fault and I had released myself of all the guilt and shame associated with it. This kind of sexual abuse and trauma was more common than we liked to be honest with ourselves and others about. I witnessed a few people along this journey who had been impacted by these same unfortunate events, and even worse cases that continued to be etched into our brains to keep as a secret. We find ourselves in a cycle that affects our mental state and can overflow into other aspects of our lives negatively.

What I realized after all this time was that our loved ones were the people who took the brunt end of our frustrations when we didn't seek help. It was important to be intentional about making a difference. Often, we say we want things to change and be different but don't hold ourselves accountable for making the choice that align with it. I had to acknowledge that things would forever be broken until we identified it as a pain point and chose to stand up to it and be the change we wanted to see. It wasn't easy and it was uncomfortable for most people involved. However, we owed it to ourselves and our families to not project the same painful inflictions on the future generation.

One of the most painful choices I had to make during this process was understanding my choice to not be in my parents' presence directly affected my ability to love on my grandmother.

The wall of protection and the time and energy I had already contributed to my healing would have all been in vain. Why? Because as soon as I crossed that threshold, I would have reverted to the little girl and not the strong, empowered woman I had grown into. For me, it wasn't worth sacrificing my peace of mind and joy. Sometimes, standing your ground on your peace of mind breaks your heart, but it was only temporary. It would have caused me to backslide into old habits and ways of doing things by sacrificing my peace by pleasing everybody.

It was a hard choice, but necessary. I challenge others to find that kind of strength to not allow others to guilt you into portraying that everything is fine. Stand in your truth.

Everything I felt was my truth, and I was allowed to feel it. He told me he admired my strength and appreciated the shared perspective. We talked about how inspiring it would be when I finished writing my book to encourage people to heal for real. I told him I was still working on my book, and when I go back and read different parts at times, I am amazed at how God works! I write when I feel a strong urge and, in the Spirit, so when I look it over later, I am honestly inspired even more to complete it. I just keep thinking about how blessed people will be to see that you can survive and thrive after trauma.

We wished each other well until the next session.

NOVEMBER 2022 SESSION:

I was looking forward to this session as things were still scattered in my mind. I started looking forward to 2023 and wondering what the way ahead without therapy looked like for me. I had confidence and faith that God would continue to carry me through as He had up to now.

I had grown accustomed to my therapy sessions because it was my comfort that I had found in knowing he was there to reassure or redirect me, whichever was necessary. I liked having that to look forward to, and realizing that would end caused me a little anxiety.

I was open and honest about these feelings with my therapist, who believed I would continue to do just fine with the new foundation I had started building on. I told him one of the things that was necessary to my growth was realizing a lot of things were built on flawed foundations. I must be truthful in saying that not everything was bad, but I needed to make a conscious, critical choice at a time when I was at a crossroads. The best decision I made was to break down every flawed brick that was causing our foundation to be unstable. In doing this, it allowed me to open my heart and mind to new possibilities and a brighter future for my kids and the generations ahead. That, I am completely excited about because they have a better chance at the beginning when they are the most vulnerable to be solid as they grow older.

I don't take the decision or their destiny lightly and that was what gave me the strength to show up over and over for these sessions. I wanted to be the best version of myself for my family before I left this world. I wanted them to know that I felt they deserved that, and so did I.

We go through so much, and a lot may be outside of our control. However, we need to be intentional about taking control of what we can so we can make a difference where it counts. I am thankful I made this choice before it was too late, because now, I am really living and loving myself and my family the way we all deserve to be loved. It was one of the BEST things I had ever experienced in my life.

While I know I can't change my past, I am fully capable of making sure my future is better. We truly triumph over him by the blood of the Lamb and by the word of our testimony, as the Bible says in Revelation. We can walk with our head held high, knowing this and walking in that victory!

My therapist was grateful for the talk and let me know my feelings were natural, but as we know, all things end. He assured me that if I wanted to do another session in the new year, that would be OK, but he was looking forward to all the great things that would come from this. He believed strongly that many would be blessed as he had said many times before.

We laughed quite a bit on the call and made sure to thank each other, for we both had been blessed in crossing paths. I told him he was the real MVP because he had stuck this out with me, and it had been over a year. I loved the fact that he wouldn't tell me what I wanted to hear and held me accountable for true change by challenging me to dig deep. I explained it had been a difficult journey for me until this point because sharing this and discussing with loved ones and even friends could be hard. Not only because it was a controversial topic but because it was hard to decipher "truth" when there were emotions and genuine love involved as it had a potential to cloud judgment.

I needed a professional from the outside looking in to really help me sort through all the trauma, pain, anxiety and every other emotion that had built up over the years with no bias. I needed to know what I had to do to truly forgive and move on with my life, understanding I should not worry myself with the things I couldn't control. It was easier said than done, but it was very real and necessary to commit to doing this. You must really be dedicated to do the work and I could say I was here for it, and I had done it!

He agreed and assured me he had enjoyed the talks and even learned some things along the way from me. We both appreciated the laughs and the journey. As the session ended, we wished each other well and a good night until next time.

DECEMBER SESSION:

As the December session came closer, I had a whirlwind of emotions, knowing we were nearing the end of our therapy sessions. I remember having a few questions for myself, but also truly reflecting on my journey over the past fifteen months. It was crazy how things could shift and turn so suddenly and shake you to your core, so much so, it all seems unfamiliar. The blessing was, when you reached your absolute lowest point in your life, the only way to go was up.

I remembered thinking how proud of myself I was because I had decided for ME, and I saw it through, despite how uncomfortable and unfamiliar it was to me. There were good times and rough moments along the way on this journey, but I did not quit, stop, or settle… I stepped and continued to do so until the last session.

I wondered if I was truly ready to continue this journey into 2023, therapy free. I got a little anxious and giving myself a pep talk that I was built for this. I convinced myself that I could always pivot if I needed to and come back to therapy if necessary. I honestly felt a bittersweet feeling as the session got closer because I didn't know how it would end or what to say to my therapist.

I tried to go backward on what my therapist and I had agreed to regarding a session a month. I told him we should schedule 2 more for December, once a week, up to the week before Christmas, so I could make sure I was ready to move forward on my own. He said he understood and that was fine if I wanted to do that.

During the session, I remember thanking him sincerely for walking this journey with me. I explained I had learned so much about myself and experienced my truth like never before. While it was painful at times, I found my true purpose in this, which was most important. I expressed much gratitude for him sticking through this with me and always being willing to challenge me to see things from a different perspective and validating that it was OK for me to feel what I feel. Never in my life had I felt more in tune with myself than now.

I expressed how proud I was that I saw this decision through because it had been life changing. He encouraged me to continue to be who I was born to be, no matter what. He told me he really enjoyed walking this journey with me and was looking forward to reading my book, which he believed would bless so many people.

I knew because this was what God wanted me to do. I had to press forward, understanding that even if it just blessed one person, I'd accomplished what I'd set out to do.

It was a blessing to know that you were loved and chosen by God, and I once was the one lost sheep that wandered off and God saw fit to leave the flock of ninety-nine to save me. I owed God everything, and while I didn't believe I could ever fully repay Him, the least I could do was fulfill His will.

It was a blessing to be a blessing. I wanted someone to see my strength and understand that God's love, grace, and mercy were the reason they saw that light in me. God was so intentional, and He loved us enough to be the strength we needed to be a beacon of light in such a dark world we lived in today.

He hadn't brought me through all I had overcome to keep it to myself. God expected His children to be a blessing to others when we could, and I wouldn't let Him down. It was bigger than me, and the fact that I knew there were so many people who would be blessed by my testimony, I had to do this. God could use anyone, and I think it was important that people knew the power and strength He could and would provide to us in our time of need.

He acknowledged everything I said and encouraged me to keep being blessed and a blessing, and advised he would schedule the next session. We wished each other well until the next time we spoke.

He sent over the session request for the second session in December and I attempted to accept it and ran into an error message. I didn't think much of it and decided I would come back to it later. Over the course of the next few days, I tried to accept the session so I could add it to my calendar and continued to receive the error message. I decided to message him to let him know I was having a hard time accepting the request, which I'd never experienced before. He deleted the request and resent it to me hoping that would resolve it and I continued to get the same error message. We agreed to continue to try a few more times, and even the next day or so, to no avail. Finally, he directed me to contact my insurance because it must be something out of his control.

It's hard to explain, but when you experience God, you just know everything happens for a reason and with intention. I had such a calm feeling about not being able to accept the session request from my therapist. I felt a strong unction that reassured me I was ready for this next phase. I had experienced this feeling multiple times before, when God was preparing me to walk out of one season and into a new one.

While I had all these questions and thoughts flooding my mind before the last session in December, none of that mattered. It was reflection time between me and God. I was so thankful I had given my therapist his flowers on that last call by thanking him and assuring him I was healed and whole, which was my goal from the beginning.

I remember looking at this season ending as I had looked at other seasons in my life. It was never a good time to say goodbye or see you later. If we had it our way, we would never rip off the band aid. No matter how much time we have, we would always want more.

I felt this way when my husband and I loss our firstborn. I used to drown in my tears, wishing and wondering if I had one more day, one more week, one more month or even years with him with the same result, would it be easier? Would it not hurt so bad? Would it hurt more because of a deeper bond and more time and memories created? At some point in my life, I had to stop doing that to myself because I was just breaking myself down to an even deeper and darker place. I learned to be thankful for the time I was blessed on this side with him and trust that God's timing is the best timing.

At the end of the day, no matter how much I wish and wonder on a would've, could've, and should've, it wouldn't change what actually was. I learned to focus on counting my blessings instead of my burdens. They both exist, and I can live, learn, and love in and through the lessons. God knew the time was up and saved me from dragging it out and changing the direction He had planned for me on The Highway to Healing.

The lesson I learned in this season of my life was that It Is What It Is... Until You Do Something Different. I was tired of looking in the mirror at this broken-hearted "little girl" in a grown woman's body.

To everyone on the outside, I had it all together. Truth was, I was hiding so much pain inside. I was broken in so many places of my life, I started not to recognize the me I saw in the mirror.

The fact was, I was not OK but was still trying to pour from an empty cup. It was so draining; I started to just exist and not really live. I thought about all the encouraging words and scriptures I had given to so many others over the years. Tears escaped me uncontrollably because who was going to be there for me to pick up the broken pieces? I needed help, but didn't know who could help me. I was so worried about everybody else and how they would feel, I neglected my own needs. Depression is real. The feeling of loneliness even when you are surrounded by people is real. Believing you are unworthy of God's love, or anyone else's, is real. All these things fester and have you thinking life would be better off without you if you let it.

I had to put everything out there this time around because I didn't know how my story would end. I made a commitment to God that I was giving my mind, body and soul this next round, and whatever it took, I wouldn't let Him down. I meant that with EVERYTHING in me with my prayer being, "Yes and amen!"

My "something different" was therapy because it helped me to see me the way God sees me. It helped me understand myself better. It helped me embrace my truth for what it is and not for what others wanted me to believe. I got a chance to take a step back and love the me God created me to be! I know my worth and what I bring to the table. I see things clearer than I ever have before. Now, I have experienced the strength that so many others saw in me over the years.

I must mention the helpful part for me was understanding the importance of unpacking the trauma and the why, acknowledging that sometimes we may never fully understand the "why" from the people who hurt us or from traumatic events. Learning how to be OK and making the choice to press forward anyway was hard for me in the beginning.

My therapist was amazed at where I was in the healing

process as I had already had multiple hard conversations with the ones who had contributed to my trauma. He advised a few things he would typically use to help others get the confidence to step out had already been done. In this, he was happy to help me on the journey and was confident I was going to be OK. This gave me a sense of peace because I felt all over the place and didn't know if any of the steps I had taken made any difference.

Truth was, we needed to challenge ourselves to intentionally take time out to extend grace to ourselves and give a pat on our own backs for small and big accomplishments. It takes a lot of courage, strength, and will power among so many other things to be dedicated to the work required to heal for real.

Therapy helped me understand the importance of having, setting, and enforcing boundaries, identifying triggers, filtering through my pain, and gaining better control of my anxiety. It was reinforced that my life was my own and I had the power to pivot and change paths to align with my purpose. This could include me knowing when to take a step back, readjust, and always being willing to draw new lines in the sand, if necessary, unapologetically.

A big lesson I learned was that it was OK to acknowledge what happened and be aware. However, it was just as important to live in the moment and appreciate what you had in front of you.

Often, we lose sight of what was right in front of us by getting caught up in the past and what was behind us. At the end of it all, faith without works is dead, so if you're not willing to do the work, you'll never win!

The focus in my sessions from day one was to heal for real. Everything up to that point was not working and I was over it. I wanted to be free from myself, certain expectations from others, and especially, from the battle in my mind. The focus was about what I could and needed to do for myself to break this cycle of generational curses.

God dealt with me about me over the course of the therapy sessions. He did allow a veil to come off my eyes a little while before I started counseling, and that was a very painful part of the process as well. When you finally get to see the people you love and call family and friends for who they REALLY are, it's life changing. It can be for the good or an adjustment that will shift your entire world as you knew it. The great news is that we deserve that truth. We should want to see the authentic versions of the people we deal with. It allows us to know what to do and how to handle them moving forward.

"It is what it is… until you do something different."
~ Shae Pratcher ~

Chapter 16
The Long Handle Spoon Approach

Since I'd committed to my healing journey, I'd adapted an alternative coping mechanism from "Fake it Until You Make It" to "The Long Handle Spoon Approach". I found it to be comforting along the way.

It came up in many of my therapy sessions after I grew tired of being disappointed, let down, unsatisfied, and discouraged with the consistent disregard for the depths of my pain. I needed a new way of thinking. I wanted to feel better but still make sure God was pleased with whatever decision I made. It was not OK for people to make choices that worked for them, resulting in me just accepting them. At some point, I needed to take the ball back in my court and take the shot!

We give people too much room to dictate and determine how they can deal with us. So, the "Long Handle Spoon" was used when you needed to put distance between you and others to create clear-cut boundaries on how you are willing to deal with each other.

The first problem was realizing I didn't have any boundaries, so I needed to establish some. I was raised to do as I was told, and there was no opportunity to discuss how I felt. When this happens, you take it into adulthood and can either be very quiet and conform often OR you become the total opposite and are very vocal and opinionated about everything.

When emotions have been disregarded for so long, you learn to disregard or take on other people's emotions. A cycle of unhealthy choices can flow from this way of living.

The Long Handle Spoon was something I carried in my toolbox and used as needed. No one was exempt. I would acknowledge, respect, and abide by your boundaries, and I expected the same in return.

In the event our relationship didn't exemplify this exchange, then I would exercise using the long handle spoon. The length of said spoon depended on what was necessary for me to retain my level of peace, joy, and happiness at all times. I made a choice that I would intentionally protect my peace. The way I looked at it, if I pulled out the long handle spoon, you would still eat, but it would be at a distance, and not at my table. The blessing was that you would still eat, and therefore, wouldn't starve.

The Long Handle Spoon Approach allows distance, whether great or small, and I was OK with this, whether you were or not, because I decide what is healthy and what is not for me.

No more forced relationships. No more faking it. No more just going along to get along. No more suffering in silence. I'm taking a stand for ME, unapologetically, and you should do the same.

The distance of the long handle spoon is determined by your actions.

Warning: Be careful with this approach because manipulators and deceivers in or around your circle can feel when you pull away. They do what they need to do or say what they feel you want to hear to keep you close enough to where they can still control you. So, they think…

Once you learn how to navigate the long handle spoon, you can bend it around corners and even stretch it along highways. The best part is you hold the handle and control who gets fed from it.

Chapter 17
Power In The U-Turn

The most powerful decision I'd made in my life, aside from accepting Jesus as my Lord and Savior, was choosing ME! I had to first acknowledge that I wasn't OK with the me I saw in the mirror. Even when I started on this healing journey, I still stated my why was for my husband and kids.

My therapist allowed me to hold this stance for a few sessions before calling me to the carpet. He said, "I get that thinking about your family helped you come to terms with deciding to seek help. However, you need to realize you didn't just do this for them, but you're doing it for *you*. That has to be the motivator because until now, part of the problem was everything you've done has been to please others."

That changed my way of thinking because it was true. I began re-evaluating my reasons and establishing a solid foundation for my future... our future. The next question was, why are you taking this step? Simply put, I was tired of looking at the same broken parts, wishing, hoping, and praying for them to be fixed to no avail.

Another question that followed was, "What do you want to accomplish at the end of the journey with therapy?"

My reply was, "I want to heal for real so I can be the best version of myself for my family. I want to be a better woman, wife, mother, sister, friend, and woman of God when it's all said and done."

I learned that what helped me to change was being intentional about taking the action to heal! It required me to put in some serious mental work. I had to relive some of the most painful parts of my past to even consider perseverance. It wasn't easy, it wasn't quick, but it was worth it!

The hard part was recognizing I had no boundaries established for anyone in my life. People crossed lines, upset me, used and abused me because there were no expectations for them to respect. I didn't feel safe or secure and didn't recognize it initially.

It was hard hearing my therapist use words like "sexually abused" and "molested" as well as "you were victimized at a young age". It felt like he was using harsh curse words at first. I had always used different terms to describe what happened to me. He had to explain to me we can't move forward without first acknowledging and calling it what it is. At the end of the day, these are the facts that are difficult to discuss but necessary to get to the end goal, which was to heal for real.

I had to reestablish what safety looked like for me. He asked what the relationships were like in real time today and if we all still associated and visited each other. At that time, the answer was yes, we all still interacted and saw each other less often than we used to, but still often. He explained to me what had happened was that I'd learned to function in a dysfunctional situation. It was unfortunate and not impossible, but would be very hard to heal still operating the same way and in that environment.

At that point, I had already made the choice to block my

father due to him not respecting the boundaries I attempted to establish. I acknowledged I could understand why he was advising me I needed to really think about the environment and if it was safe and healthy for myself and my family, considering all things. I had to make a choice to operate in what made me comfortable because it was what I was used to, or to make a change and focus on my healing. I had to accept the fact that I couldn't do both and obtain the end goal I had hoped for.

It was at that point, I chose ME for once over what everybody else wanted. I understood that making this choice would cause some people to be upset and uncomfortable, but I had to look at my foundation and realize it was falling because it was flawed. I needed to focus on building a new foundation for my family so things didn't continue to fester and follow them all their life. I decided that my safe haven was my house. I was committed to utilizing the long handle spoon and allowing the distance to remain between my father and myself. It was best for me to focus on myself with no distractions or manipulation. I chose to keep him blocked and keep the lines of communication open with my mother.

I didn't warn my father prior to blocking him because I didn't feel he deserved it. I felt like I had been very clear and direct in asking him not to text me. I also explained that I was working on healing and needed some time to do this. He said he understood but turned around less than two days later and texted me anyway, then called and left a voicemail that he knew I asked him not to, but he had to. He further advised me that if I didn't respond, that was OK, but he just had to send them. I decided I didn't want to receive them or see them pop up even, so I blocked him. I felt like I was being forced to do something I didn't want to, and I was determined not to get pulled back into that unhealthy cycle.

I was committed to the boundaries I had set, and he had overstepped, and it required action. I understood I couldn't change people, nor was I trying to do that, so I did what was best for me. He could continue to send them, and I didn't have to see them.

My mother and I had some conversations, but we didn't discuss the details of what my father and I had talked about in my driveway right away. I didn't feel obligated to discuss it because I didn't feel it would make a difference.

In speaking with my therapist, he made me realize the "action part" of my healing was a constant choice. He would ask me direct questions regarding how I handled a situation regarding speaking and standing up for myself. Sometimes, I explained to him I didn't speak up because it wasn't worth entertaining. He challenged me to see it differently. He advised that as a child, my voice was silenced and that sometimes could translate into being passive aggressive. He explained that was the old Shae's way of handling things and that Shae was gone. He encouraged me to speak up, even if it was me reiterating a point. I needed to express how I felt. Sometimes it was about standing up for myself and it would become more natural to do when the time was right.

I ended up letting my mom know I blocked my father and the reason I had done it. I was very honest and explained he had a total disregard for my boundaries and no respect for them. I shared with her how it made me feel when he disrespected my boundaries and that I felt like I was a kid all over again, being forced to do something I didn't want to do. I explained to her that I was in counseling and working on healing and I didn't need anything standing in the way of that. I wasn't sure if the block would be temporary or long term, but I was going to let God lead me on that. I also shared with her at that point the details of the discussion he and I had in my driveway and that it left me feeling uneasy. She assured me she understood my reason for blocking him and wanted to stay out of the middle. Shortly after, we ended the call amicably.

This was another win for me because I took a stand and

didn't back down. Although the conversation was uncomfortable for me to have, I had it. This was something I would not have done prior to me embarking on this healing journey.

With this boundary set in place, I made the choice to discontinue any trips to their house to fully emerge and commit myself to my healing journey.

The next painful part involved me being willing to process the details from the trauma with a complete stranger. I had to trust that he could help me break things down in such a way, it would help me to ultimately make better decisions for my future. Again, I chose to put my fears to the side and put my trust in the professional who dedicated the time and effort to helping me up to that point.

A great deal of time was spent in this phase. It took some time to break it all down, but this was an intricate part in my healing. No rush. Session after session, we broke it all the way down.

Measuring the post-trauma growth was the most rewarding! Once I could talk about my traumatic experiences without it hurting so bad, I knew I was on my way out of the dark. There was a time when I was so anxious, easily worked up and triggered at just the thought of my past. Then, I entered the season where I could talk through it repeatedly without my heart aching and feeling so broken. I was able to acknowledge what happened, but not be activated into feeling like I must put up walls and shut down. I realize the growth and I count every win, no matter how small or big! I'd come a long way and I'd finally chosen ME!

I'd learned some valuable lessons through the years. When people say, "Everything that glitters isn't gold," this is so true. People can and will control the version of them you see. It's the very people you think have it all together that are scrambled and a "hot mess" at the very core.

I had to recognize that for a very long time, I'd been viewing the world through traumatic lenses. This was due to me experiencing trauma and not getting any help for so long.

People have asked me over the years, "Why do you think your mom stayed?"

My honest answer was, "She thought about her finances and future, and it included him in it."

While my mom made some selfless decisions for us growing up, the choice to stay with a man who molested their biological daughter for seven years was not one of them. The decision was directly about their image. I'd played this back in my mind thousands of times to try to see it from another perspective and how she could've possibly validated her decision. I'd never been able to understand it or make sense of it. Although, in conversation with my mom to this day, she believes and says, "I made the choice God wanted me to make, or He wouldn't have let me make it."

I didn't agree. We all had free will to make the choices we wanted and there were consequences that derived from them. Due to the close relationship we all had, and the expectations set and understood during our upbringing, it sheltered me from important things. I do believe if I had been more comfortable speaking up, I wouldn't have suffered in silence for seven years. I believe I would have had it in me to take a stand for myself and my own family before I was in my thirties. Since I had to suck it up and deal with it as a child, I learned how to operate normally in a dysfunctional situation and didn't even realize it.

My husband was made aware of everything that happened to me prior to us getting married. His love for me even allowed him to grow accustomed to the dysfunction. He learned to grow comfortable being uncomfortable in an unfortunate situation that he shouldn't have had to for so many years of our marriage. Counseling and therapy helped me to see through a clearer lens. They helped me to identify my triggers and trace them back to the source, which was my childhood trauma. I'm very vocal now and that stems from a lack of being able to speak up or out growing up.

I am no longer the same angry, broken, or bitter girl/woman anymore. I acknowledged there were some broken parts of me and was determined to go in and come out better on the other side. Not only did I learn so much about myself going through the process, but along my journey, I found HEALING. I experienced TRUE HEALING, and it was the best thing/choice I made for me, my husband, and our kids. They now can experience the BEST parts of me because I'm no longer broken in those areas that I once was. I give all the praise, honor, and glory to God because HE is the only reason I was able to make it through!

Sometimes in life, we try to take shortcuts. Along the journey, we can be guilty of manipulating our way to the top by trying to go above, around, and under where we need to. Honestly, some things are only accomplished by going THROUGH it! Along the way on this highway to healing, I found my path to the promise and my purpose.

As I look over my life, I've had to endure some real pain and everlasting trauma, but I'm not a victim. I had to grow up spiritually or I never would have survived. I'm thankful my grandmother introduced the Lord to me when I needed Him the most. I never let go of His hand.

At such a young age, I learned I had to be my own advocate. Although I didn't understand everything that encompassed at the time, with God's help, I did it! I stand here today in His strength, not mine. I know that according to my past and the statistics, I should not be who I am today. But God! Understand that this journey on "The Highway to Healing" has been long and hard. There were times when reverting to the "dead ends" and old habits and ways of thinking I found comfort in for so long seemed ideal. Why? Because the investment, commitment, and time it took to allow the process to actually work required you to make the choice of a lifetime.

We are living in a generation and time where we expect and want everything now! Healing is something that takes time and can't be done overnight. It took me getting tired of looking at the broken parts of me to make that *choice* to make this *change*. It's the *best* thing I could've done for *me*.

For once in my life, I put ME and what I not only *wanted* but what I *deserved* first. Sometimes, we can absolutely give the best parts of us to all the wrong people. This can be family, friends, enemies, and everyone in between.

Don't read this book feeling sorry for me because I don't live in that place anymore. Read this and be encouraged enough to find the same strength in YOU to choose YOU! It's my journey and all the life experiences that led me on the path to "The Highway to Healing." It's these same struggles where I found my strength that contributed to the woman I am today! I have no regrets.

As painful as it has been, if I had to go through it all again to get to the promise and fulfill my purpose, I would. It's because I've learned and believe that our tests and trials are BIGGER than us. I'm the willing vessel. I'm the one that continues to raise her hand and say, "Lord, I'll go," and "Lord, You can use me." My prayer is still "Yes and Amen."

The intent is not to highlight all the things that went wrong but to be completely transparent about this God glow you see! I want to give the credit where it is due. The "ME" you SEE is because of the light and God in me! I experienced a lot of *losses in my life*, but the *wins* make it *worth* it.

I serve a God who is intentional about His children. I understand this so every part of my journey, He has used to be a blessing to someone else. I always say, "It's a blessing to be a blessing."

I'm not talking about these materialistic things that mean absolutely nothing when you leave this world. I'm talking about sharing what you've learned to try to bless someone else in such a way its life changing. You bless people BIG when you are obedient and do it God's way. This requires you to continuously pray, "Lord, less of me and more of you!"

When you mean it, you get it, and you know when you're in the right posture. You do what needs to be done, despite what you feel like doing. You become serious about your Father's business and count your blessings, not your burdens.

Chapter 18
The Highway To Healing Exit

A long my journey on "The Highway to Healing", I gained so much more than I ever loss. I had to "Glance Back to Get Back" to the bigger message by acknowledging "What Happened?" during "The Exchange" and "The Return". I developed a coping mechanism and attitude of "It Is What It Is", not realizing I was only surviving. It wasn't until I had my firstborn, "Little Man 606", and experienced "The Breakdown" that I realized I needed to slow down and take a new route to BREAKTHROUGH.

In doing this, my relationship with God grew stronger and on a much deeper level. It was in that place that I learned I had three choices in life and God challenged me to confirm if I was going to "Stop, Settle, or Step?" When I cried out to God and decided I was going to Step, despite all the tests and trials I had experienced, the journey elevated. This triggered a reroute to a "Faith Fuel Stop." My new posture and prayer were and still is, "Yes and Amen!"

I learned quickly that this decision didn't make the enemy happy and the "Detour is in The Details". I was challenged in my mind, body, and spirit even more than before.

During this dark and difficult time was when I realized my husband was always right there, and it had always been "Just Us", in and through it all! It was then I realized my "Trauma Triggered" at different times and I wasn't in control as much as I had thought. It was at that point I knew I had to face the facts and start confronting them head on, one by one.

"The Sit Down" was just a setup for "The Stand Up", which was where I found much of my strength! I had to do those things if I ever expected to truly heal.

These hard truths uncovered in those conversations with the ones closest to me who had let me down, hurt, disappointed, and failed to protect me, needed to hear how it had impacted me well into my adulthood. This empowered me to take back the control I had lost over myself to feel and express it freely. I made a choice after that painful part to seek professional help. It was only through this intentional healing process I learned a way to adapt to a new perspective.

The truth was, "It Is What It Is… Until You Do Something Different." Doing the same thing expecting different results is truly insanity. You will find yourself stuck in a cycle, battling with yourself and them, and no one wins. I gained a new tool along the way called "The Long Handle Spoon Approach." This tool has been key on my journey on "The Highway to Healing" because it allows me to create healthy boundaries and control the distance between myself and others. It's necessary. I learned that the biggest roadblock that was keeping me from my healing was failing to establish AND enforce healthy and safe boundaries.

Once I made this choice and change my road to recovery was close! The last stop was me recognizing the "Power in The U-Turn". This required me looking in the mirror and saying, "You not only need to do this for your family, but YOU deserve to do it for YOU! People should get the WHOLE HEALED version of YOU not the HALF HEALED with HOLES version. There is SO much POWER in YOU CHOOSING YOU!"

Don't grow comfortable just trying to survive when God has called you to thrive! I challenge YOU to choose YOU and heal for real!

"They say hurt people, hurt people. So, in my mind, HEALED people should help people. That's my hope and the purpose in sharing my testimony. Be blessed."
~Shae Pratcher~

AUTHOR'S NOTE & ACKNOWLEDGMENT

First and foremost, I want to thank God for never leaving nor forsaking me. He is the reason I persevered because, even when I wanted to throw in the towel over the years, He wouldn't let me. He never gave up on me and continued to extend His love, grace, and mercy toward me throughout my entire life.

I truly owe God EVERYTHING but understand that all I can do is be dedicated to fulfilling His Will for my life, which is the reason I embarked on this journey. The only thing that remained consistent and worked was putting my faith in God and trusting that HE would bring me through. God helped me to truly understand that this is not about me and allowed me to heal in order to help others, and that's what I will continue to do.

To my husband, Mazio Pratcher, you are simply AMAZING! You have always loved me, flaws and all, even through my imperfections. I didn't know how broken I truly was before I met you. It was definitely through me choosing to love you I learned more than I ever imagined I would. Above all else, you taught me the importance of living in my truth. Our marriage isn't perfect, and we have been tested more times than I can count. The good news is that we have persevered and there is no one else I would prefer to share the rest of my life with. Thank you for loving and supporting me through all the seasons and everything that each one has encompassed. It's because of your support that I am a better woman overall. Sincerely, thank you from the depths of my heart.

To my children, Braylen, Jaylen, Janiyah and Justus, please

know that each of you have and hold a special place in my heart. I thank each one of you for teaching me something different about myself year after year. The reason I decided to heal for real was because I had each of you in mind and decided that YOU deserve the best version of ME. I want you each to understand that God can and will keep and sustain YOU in and through ANY storm. Be encouraged and hold on to your faith, especially when things get hard. While this assignment wasn't an easy one, it was one worth every tear I shed. The result is that I am no longer broken in those places I once was, which allows me to love y'all even better than before. Why? Because I am healed and whole. I love you, and it is my prayer that each of you will be as intentional in walking out your purpose as you grow older.

Michael Valdes, my therapist, YOU are the MVP. I did not know what to expect when I started on this highway to healing. There were so many things I was not sure about. You were committed to the journey and did not let up not one session. I appreciate your honesty, professional advice, challenges, and the many laughs that we shared during our fifteen months together. Your dedication to ensuring I kept the end goal to heal for real at the forefront was valued. You helped me to gain a new perspective while challenging me to dig deeper than the surface to really get to the heart of the matter.

Ultimately, I learned so much more about myself, the reasons why I see people the way I do, the importance of establishing and enforcing boundaries, and how to embrace my truth unapologetically. I know I can't change people, nor should that ever be a focus. I have the right to make choices that are healthy for me and my family and should not feel bad about this. You reinforced for me that everyone is entitled to their opinion and has a right to make their own choices. These choices always have consequences, and we need to live with them. I just want to say THANK YOU for listening, allowing me to feel and express my truth without judging me and always being ready to reassure or redirect me, respectively. Your advice and voice will always play over in my mind when I am having those tough conversations and faced with making hard decisions. I am forever changed, and I must thank you publicly for this.

Auntie April a.k.a. my TT in love... where do I start? We have been attached for a good portion of my life, and for many assignments. You are so many things and mean SO much to me, it almost feels like there aren't the perfect words to say, but I will try.

You are one of the most kindhearted, genuine, dedicated, and loving people I know. You have supported me in EVERY major and minor milestone I have celebrated. From the music to the radio shows to this book and EVERYTHING in between, you have been SOLID and consistent. I appreciate you being my accountability partner in every aspect of my life. We have laughed, cried, and prayed through so many countless obstacles and opportunities. You have encouraged me and poured back into my cup more times than I can recall. I am thankful for all the seasons that we have shared and don't take any of it for granted. You understand and get me on an entirely different scale. The impact you have made and continue to make in my life is truly irreplaceable. Thank YOU for simply being YOU and I can only hope that I am as big of a blessing to you as you are to me and my family.

Eboni West A.K.A. my BESTIE! We have been rocking together for over twenty YEARS and our sisterhood and friendship is like no other! You are truly one of a kind and the one I have entrusted to share my deepest secrets with to my greatest accomplishments. You have loved me unconditionally through some of the lowest and most difficult times of my life and I am FOREVER THANKFUL for this. You have extended grace to me over the years when I shut down and shut everyone out and you welcome me back with open arms, always picking up where we left off. You extend a helping hand whenever and wherever I need it. You see a need and fulfill it without ever needing an invitation. You have one of the purest and most generous souls I have ever known. Nobody can give me feedback and new perspective like you have given to me. We have had so many conversations, shed tears, empathized and sympathized with each other many times over the years. Thank YOU for always loving, supporting, and caring for me and my family the way you do. I LOVE YOU and value the sisterhood that we have.

Bobbie Clark - Little did I know, our connection would change my life forever. You've taught me the true impact of experiencing people in a selfless way and I'll always love you for that. I appreciate the sisterhood and friendship I have found in you. It's been consistent and genuine, even through distance. I'm forever thankful and blessed that our paths crossed. I admire your strength and drive in life to persevere, in spite of whatever it throws your way. Keep being you, sis, with much love and gratitude. I love you, and it's up from here!

Chasity A.K.A. CHAS... My GIRL! You have been a pivotal part of this journey for me, and I MUST publicly thank YOU! Writing a book was something very new for me and you extended patience throughout the entire process! I look to you as the SME in this arena and you exceeded my expectations from encouragement to empathizing with me to connecting me with your network of professionals for editing, proofreading and formatting. You are so sweet and genuine and always have been willing to lend a helping hand and share the knowledge you have gained along the way. Thanks for making yourself available for hours on end and holding me accountable to seeing this through. YOU are such an inspiration and I pray many blessings for you and your family! Oh, and by the way... I am working on launching that podcast, that's next! (Insider)

Crystal Collier of Crystallized Editing LLC - You are AMAZING, and I had to shout you out for being a big part of the EDITING process! This journey has been something NEW and being connected with the right people is KEY! You unlocked a new perspective in me with your feedback and I pray that your craft is blessed beyond measure, exceedingly and abundantly above your highest expectation! I highly recommend your services, and please know, I appreciated your insights and professionalism. Check my girl out if you need an editor at Edits ByCrystal@gmail.com!

Last but certainly not least on my list... To ALL the trauma survivors out there, THANK YOU for being the inspiration and reason for MY WHY in sharing my story. We suffer in silence, thinking our story doesn't matter or won't make a difference, and that's what keeps us stuck. We are done settling with surviving when God has called us to thrive! You owe it to yourself to heal for real so that YOU TOO can be the best version of YOU! Thank you in advance for taking a stance.

www.ingramcontent.com/pod-product-compliance
Lightning Source LLC
Chambersburg PA
CBHW050526170426
43201CB00013B/2105